## DATE DUE

Library Store     Peel Off Pressure Sensitive

# Clara
# Barton

Recent Titles in
Contributions in Women's Studies

Sex, Abortion and Unmarried Women
*Paul Sachdev*

Mules and Dragons: Popular Culture Images in the Selected Writings
of African-American and Chinese-American Women Writers
*Mary E. Young*

Women, Community, and the Hormel Strike of 1985–86
*Neala J. Schleuning*

Edith Wharton's Prisoners of Consciousness: A Study of Theme
and Technique in the Tales
*Evelyn E. Fracasso*

Mothers and Work in Popular American Magazines
*Kathryn Keller*

Ideals in Feminine Beauty: Philosophical, Social, and Cultural
Dimensions
*Karen A. Callaghan, editor*

The Stone and the Scorpion: The Female Subject of Desire in the
Novels of Charlotte Brontë, George Eliot, and Thomas Hardy
*Judith Mitchell*

The Several Worlds of Pearl S. Buck: Essays Presented at a
Centennial Symposium, Randolph-Macon Woman's College,
March 26–28, 1992
*Elizabeth J. Lipscomb, Frances E. Webb, and Peter Conn, editors*

Hear Me Patiently: The Reform Speeches of Amelia Jenks Bloomer
*Anne C. Coon, editor*

Nineteenth-Century American Women Theatre Managers
*Jane Kathleen Curry*

Textual Escap(e)ades: Mobility, Maternity, and Textuality in
Contemporary Fiction by Women
*Lindsey Tucker*

The Repair of the World: The Novels of Marge Piercy
*Kerstin W. Shands*

# CLARA BARTON

## *In the Service of Humanity*

## DAVID H. BURTON

*Contributions in Women's Studies, Number 148*
*Jon L. Wakelyn, Series Adviser*

GREENWOOD PRESS
Westport, Connecticut • London

Library of Congress Cataloging-in-Publication Data

Burton, David Henry.
    Clara Barton : in the service of humanity / David H. Burton.
       p.  cm.—(Contributions in women's studies, ISSN 0147–104X ;
no. 148)
    Includes bibliographical references and index.
    ISBN 0–313–28945–X (alk. paper)
    1. Barton, Clara, 1821–1912.  2. Red Cross—United States—
Biography.  3. Nurses—United States—Biography.  I. Title.
II. Series.
HV569.B3B87   1995
361.7′634′092—dc20
[B]      94–37878

British Library Cataloguing in Publication Data is available.

Library of Congress Catalog Card Number: 94–37878
ISBN: 0–313–28945–X
ISSN: 0147–104X

First published in 1995

Greenwood Press, 88 Post Road West, Westport, CT  06881
An imprint of Greenwood Publishing Group, Inc.

Printed in the United States of America

The paper used in this book complies with the
Permanent Paper Standard issued by the National
Information Standards Organization (Z39.48–1984).

10  9  8  7  6  5  4  3  2  1

**Copyright Acknowledgment**

The author and publisher gratefully acknowledge permission for use of the
following material:

William E. Barton, *The Life of Clara Barton*. 2 vols., New York: AMS Press, 1969.

For Three Generations
of Burton Women

# Contents

Preface                                             ix

1   Years to Womanhood                               1

2   Battlefield Commission                          25

3   Travels and Travail                             65

4   A New Beginning                                 81

5   The Red Cross: What It Became                   99

6   Road to Rejection                              139

7   Last Years, Last Words                         159

Bibliography                                       167

Index                                              171

# *Preface*

This life of Clara Barton is an account both sympathetic and critical. Any rendering of her work and her personality must be so styled. She enriched the lives and the memories of so many people with her courage and kindnesses, mostly common folk at home and abroad, that she was like the music of the spheres. Barton's virtues were many, not the least of which was a tenacity of purpose. To give up the fight for the chance to succor the wounded and dying on the battlefield, or to yield to the Establishment when it came to American participation in the International Red Cross, such surrenders would have been inimical to what Clara deemed the right. Clara Barton kept a clear and steady focus on what she believed justice demanded of people and no less of nations. "In the service of humanity" is therefore the central theme of this summing up of her life, her years of fruitful endeavor. To serve others, whatever the cost to herself, comes through time after time. A character trait revealed in childhood, it became overriding.

Undoubtedly heroic and wonderfully generous in her impulse to serve, Clara Barton remained self-centered and egotistical. The older she became, the less she could brook criticism or a failure to show gratitude for the good she had done. A need for honor and praise, amounting to a craving, were what she required to carry out her good works. Barton was a strange cross of saint and sinner. To say that she was much loved but often not much liked is one way to represent this dichotomy of personality. All of which adds fascination to her life and reinforces the need to approach it with equal measures of admiration and detachment. The question then arises, which are we most likely to remember: the merciful Clara Barton or the dauntless seeker after notice? Each reader must answer such a question personally. In the pages that follow the dice are not loaded. That means, of course, judgments will vary. But surely her story will leave no one indifferent to the question.

Nor can I be indifferent to the help and encouragement received from many individuals. At the Library of Congress James H. Hutson, chief of the Manuscript Division, has been especially diligent on my behalf, and Ramón Miró, also of the Library of Congress, has done valuable legwork. Wallace Dailey, curator of the Theodore Roosevelt Papers at the Houghton Library, Harvard University, and Barbara Lang of Drexel Library, Saint Joseph's University, provided me with answers and books, respectively. Frank Gerrity (who read the manuscript in its entirety), Edmund Morris and Randall Miller made useful suggestions. Friendly encouragement of a nonspecialized sort came from Francis Graham Lee, Phillip T. Smith, Robert F. Jones, Vincent A. McCarthy, Morton Jaffe, Edward G. Sutula, Chuck Patterson, Esmond Wright, and Alec Campbell. My brother's interest never flagged. Antoinette Burton was always there when I needed her advice.

A generous grant from the Faculty Research Board, Saint Joseph's University, enabled me to complete the writing of the book, and my thanks go to John Tudor, chairman of the board and to the other board members. Dan Curran's assistance in making it possible to deliver the manuscript in final form is another example of both personal and institutional support that is much appreciated.

Finally I am pleased to thank HarperCollins Publishers and AMS Press for permission to make use of material held under their copyright.

# Clara
# Barton

# — 1 —

# *Years to Womanhood*

There is something portentous in the fact that Clara Barton was born on Christmas Day, 1821, as there is, upon reflection, something sobering about the day of her death, Good Friday, 1912. During her life of four score and ten she did the Lord's work, as she understood it, exceeding every expectation her family and friends were to have for her, and emerging as one of the heroines of nineteenth-century America. Yet her most ardent admirers never claimed her as a saint, even after her passing. Clara Barton was, rather, thoroughly human: diligent with an insatiable appetite for work and for recognition; intelligent and imaginative in a willingness to dare and to defy those who stood in her way. A woman resilient of body but subject to fits of the deepest depression Clara Barton was indefatigable, yet never really happy with herself without a challenge to face. Being happy with herself may well be the key to understanding Barton's life of service and sacrifice for the cause of mankind, just as her failures may be traced to the discontent she suffered when things went poorly.

Perhaps no woman made so distinctive a mark on the history of nineteenth-century America as Clara Barton. Unlike other women of achievement who committed themselves to the cause of abolition or educational reform or female suffrage, Barton stepped boldly into what the conventions of the day dictated were male preserves: the federal bureaucracy and the world of war. In the course of events her transition from government clerk to battlefield presence was nothing less than incredible, a disbelief that fades rapidly with an account of her war work. With the coming of peace and the burial of the dead, Clara Barton needed a fresh summons to action. It came unexpectedly while she was spending time in Europe, a trip she had taken to relieve the pressure of inaction. There she learned of a new organization, the International Red Cross, with whose aims and objectives she was instinctively sympathetic. An eyewitness to its remarkable efforts to alleviate the suffering of soldiers and civilians on both sides of the Franco-Prussian War, she could only express dismay that her country was not a signatory to the Geneva Convention, the enabling act of the Red Cross. At once she set out to secure a commitment from the United States government to the principles enunciated in the Convention. Years of patient lobbying in the Senate and at the White House, an activity Barton understood and clearly relished, paid off when Washington agreed to membership. Despite her age, she was sixty-one at the time, Barton threw herself wholly into the work of the American Red Cross. As its president she managed the affairs of what was a growing agency dedicated to the service of people in need, but she never lost her enthusiasm for field work, whether at Johnstown after the flood, Galveston in the wake of the tidal wave, Cuba during the Spanish-American War, or far-off Armenia and the starving people there. Where the action was, there was Clara Barton, that is where she had to be. This was the true Clara Barton, a presence in the midst of catastrophe.

The growth of the American Red Cross, measured by its ever-expanding commitments to human welfare and its increasingly complex financial requirements, seemed to many as beyond Barton's competence to manage. Or was it advancing age making her appear inept? At eighty-three she was ousted from the presidency of the Red Cross by a combination of powerful men and women who saw, perhaps better than she, the need to transform the organization to a modern legal entity. Loss of place left Clara bitter and, more alarming, unfulfilled. In her last years she suffered much, neglected if not forgotten, bearing her cross very much alone.[1]

The early years of Clarissa Harlowe Barton, as she was christened, foretold little of what became her enduring life's work. She was born the last of five children, separated by ten years from her closest sibling. The Barton family derived from old and established New England dissenter stock. Ancestors had settled the village of North Oxford, Massachusetts, which lay about fifty miles west of Boston, early in the eighteenth century. By the time of Clara's birth the settlement had grown to a small town, whose prosperity rested on farming and milling, a prosperity in which the Barton family shared. The head of the family, Stephen Barton, and his wife, Sarah, were strong-willed individuals, a trait they surely passed on to their youngest child. For Clara her father was her first and greatest hero. The son of Dr. Stephen Barton, he was born in 1774, on the eve of the struggle for independence, and a movement the doctor strongly supported. The younger Stephen gained military experience in the Indian wars that were part of the settlement of the Northwest Territory. There he served for three years under General Mad Anthony Wayne. Drawn by a spirit of adventure and strong in his desire to help push the American frontier ever westward, Barton nonetheless returned to North Oxford when it came time to settle down and make a future for himself. The future proved to be a successful one, whether measured by personal or public models. His children tended to be industrious, studious, active, and outgoing. It was a family to be proud of, despite the shadows cast by an assortment of misfortunes.

"Captain" Barton as he liked to call himself in later years took civic responsibility seriously. He commanded the local militia, served as a selectman as well as a representative to the General Court of Massachusetts. In politics he was liberal, a good Jacksonian Democrat, and a force for constructive change, including community and industrial improvement. Raised a Baptist the captain was attracted to Universalism, a denomination with strong democratic overtones. Especially popular in rural areas, Universalism tended to dismiss the divinity of Christ and the tenet of original sin with the same stroke, proclaiming a lenient theology. For Barton the social justice side of the Christian ethic had the most appeal, including care for destitute families in and around Oxford. His means were limited but his charity a generous and genuine impulse. Strength of will was not all that he passed on to young Clara.

In many ways the captain was idealized by his youngest, yet probably his most important legacy was his loving kindness toward Clara. He was her "soldier father" as he spun tales of long-dead kinsmen who had fought on the Lancastrian side in the War of the Roses, and of his days of trial and trouble as a soldier under Mad Anthony Wayne. And he had yarns indeed to tell about Wayne himself and his daring, about the death of Tecumseh at the Battle of the Thames, how he was a signatory to the peace treaty that ended the wars. Clara was quite simply enthralled by her father, and his memory remained vivid in her mind as the years passed. In recalling him she wrote that he had taught her "next to Heaven, our highest duty was to love and serve our country and honor and support its laws."[2] His was a lasting inheritance.

Stephen Barton married Sarah Stone, a local girl of good family, in 1804. Only seventeen at the time Sarah was four months pregnant. Her temperament was altogether different from that of her husband. Her manner was abrupt, and she often lashed out at those around her. A woman quick of temper, she possessed and indulged in a knack for profanity. Sarah was every bit a hard-working housewife. She could do two days' work in one according to Clara, up well before dawn winter and summer alike. Discipline was one of her habits in raising a family, discipline which taught responsibility. No task once assigned must be left undone. Baking, cooking, sewing, and cleanliness of person and clothing were part of the household routine for Clara and her siblings. Mother Barton was, perhaps surprisingly, a determined social reformer. Her opposition to slavery was well known throughout the town, and she was even more ardent on the subject of female emancipation. Years later to a gathering of suffragists Clara recalled that she "must have been born believing in the full rights of women to all privilege and position which nature and justice accorded her. . . . When as a young woman I heard the subject discussed it seemed ridiculous that any reasonable person should question it."[3] Sarah

Barton may not have been an easy person to live with but she taught her children worthy principles to live by. When she died in 1851 Clara's diary spoke of the loneliness she felt with her mother's passing.

As the baby in the family, her older sisters and brothers, Dorothea and Sarah, Stephen and David, affectionately referred to her as Tot for she remained a little tot to them. Clara recalled the family dynamics in this way: "I had no playmates but in effect six fathers and mothers. . . . All took charge of me, all educated me according to their personal tastes. My two sisters were scholars and artistic and strove in that direction. My brothers were strong, ruddy young men, full of life and ambition."[4]

A closer look at her response to sisters and brothers shows that Clara did indeed gain something special from each. The impressions each was to have on her were lasting ones. Dorothea, or Dolly as she was called, was the oldest child, already seventeen when Clara was born. This difference in age helped to define their relationship. At first Dolly was a second mother, much concerned with doing things for baby. She was never to marry and have children of her own, but her maternal instincts were strong and Clara was the better for it. Dolly taught school for a number of years in the North Oxford area but remained "ever watchful" of her little sister. Her mental breakdown in 1827, with Clara only six years old, left Tot with a permanent scar. From 1827 until Dolly's death in 1838, her family kept Dolly's insanity a secret, as was often the way at a time when such an affliction was looked upon by many as God's curse. After all, had she not been conceived in sin! In later years Clara rarely referred to her sister's illness and became comfortable with the explanation that Dolly had died an invalid's death. But she did not forget how kind and generous Dolly had been to her, making her conscious at a very early age of the value of learning and spurring her to enlarge her world of knowledge.

Clara's elder brother, the second child, was understandably more remote from Tot as she grew up. As adults however they were very close. Named for his grandfather and father, this Stephen Barton also taught school for a while but soon discovered his true calling lay in the milling business and in public service in and around North

Oxford. After he was made a partner in the family milling enterprise he appears to have thrived. In the process he gained a reputation for sharp business practice. Then in 1851 Stephen was indicted for bank robbery. Though he was not convicted, his character remained in question and he decided to move to North Carolina. Some five years before the war between the states, he established a milling complex on the Chowan River, having sold his interest in the family business. As a Yankee in the ante-bellum South, Stephen was an anomaly and came under considerable risk once the war was underway. Clara made strenuous efforts to keep in touch with him but living in rebel territory bore down heavily on him. He died in 1865 just as the conflict was winding down.

Brother David, younger than Stephen by two years, played the role of big brother more aptly. He was always fond of Tot and took an interest in her upbringing. He encouraged in her a love of animals that stayed with her throughout her life, and taught her how to ride a horse "good as any boy." This one skill served her more than once during the Civil War. To David, Clara was completely devoted.

Sister Sally also became a school teacher before she married Vester Vassall. She was possibly too close in age to Tot to have had a discernible influence. The two sisters got on well together, reading the novels of Sir Walter Scott, their favorite author, and much English and American poetry. In adulthood they were near to one another, the more so in view of Dolly's declining condition. Sally's children had in Clara a caring and affectionate aunt.

Despite having six fathers and mothers, or perhaps because of them, Clara Barton had to develop as her own person. That she was much loved there was no doubt on her part. Yet her early childhood proved difficult. She was the little one in the family. Often she was not taken seriously in the many discussions of family matters and that tended to make her withdrawn and timid. It meant as well she suffered silently where another might have spoken out, or blurted out, her feelings. Something as prosaic as the need for a pair of new gloves, which she hesitated to ask for, caused her great worry. Equally strange, such necessities as the replacement of a well-worn dress were overlooked by her six fathers and mothers, probably because she never complained. The result was unfortunate as it reinforced in her a sense of unimportance and inadequacy.

What saved Clara from total intimidation was a keen mind: she was curious, quick to learn, and willing to show off her accomplishments as a budding scholar. School, in consequence, and in a broader sense, education, became vital to her growth if not to her very survival. The family encouraged her love of learning and took pride in her rapid progress in school. Not every New England household of the time was so disposed. The education of daughters frequently was frowned on as it did not serve the conventional roles of wife and mother. But the liberalism of the Bartons was virtually all inclusive so that Clara did not have to fight for the right to be fully schooled. Unconsciously she began to think of teaching as a possible calling, despite the persistent worry that she might be a failure because of a lack of self-confidence.

Clara was at home in the company of boys and men almost instinctively. A closeness to her "soldier father" nurtured this attitude at first, and brothers Stephen and David managed to add to her sense of ease in masculine situations. She loved to play at boys' games and did well at them. Horsemanship blended nicely with other male pastimes, including ice-skating, ball games, and romps across the meadows. When her brothers grew too old to have time to indulge her, she was able to turn to cousins Jerry and Otis Learned, boys her own age. That Clara was a tomboy greatly vexed her mother. But she pleased her mother because she never shirked her household chores, whether it was feeding the chickens, milking the cows, or watching over the lambs. Animals were her friends, and she treated them gently, as befitted a young farm girl.

When David was badly injured in a fall as the result of a barn-raising accident, Clara became his nurse and constant companion. The lad was laid up for nearly two years during which time, from her eleventh to her fourteenth year, she scarcely left his bedside. What nursing she did amounted to nothing beyond meeting his wants but she carried out such tasks with cheerful competence. Her attendance upon David as much as medical treatment helped him through dark days until his health gradually returned. Meanwhile she had wanted to join cousins who were working in the family satinet mill. With David recovered Clara went on the factory floor. Too tiny to reach the looms, Stephen had a stool built so that she might keep the spindles whirring. Such employment was to be short lived; the mill burned down shortly after she commenced working.

Clara was again without a focus, whether viewed by herself or by others who cared for her. Mother Barton was especially apprehensive. She never really understood her youngest child. But for all her brusque treatment she loved Clara and love brought on worry about her future. Partial resolution of the quandary came about when the English phrenologist, L. N. Fowler, while on a lecture tour of New England, stopped over at the Barton house. Hopeful that an examination of Clara might provide some clue as to the youngster's inner self, Sarah explained to Fowler that she was desperate to know what to do with her. Fowler's analysis of Clara's personality was remarkably astute. "She will never assert herself for herself—she will suffer wrong first—but for others she will be perfectly fearless." He then went on to advise Sarah to "throw responsibility on her. She has all the qualities of a teacher. As soon as her age will permit, give her a school to teach." And so it was that little Clara, not five feet tall and full of misgivings about herself and her abilities one day was to step into the classroom. What is singular about Fowler's assessment is not that teaching should be her calling, but that somehow he had penetrated to the inner Clara: not for herself, but for others she would be "perfectly fearless." How true that was to be. At the time, however, Clara was not so sure. She was fifteen years old and sick in bed with the mumps as she listened to Sarah's plea and Fowler's response. Years later she acknowledged the advice of this phrenologist who reasoned more like a psychologist. Her reading in phrenology, she wrote, led her to widen her attempts to understand herself, eventually leading on to a "know thyself" formula. "Know thyself has taught me in any great crisis to put myself under my own feet; bury enmity, cast ambition to the winds, ignore complaint, despise retaliation, and stand erect in the consciousness of those higher qualities that made for the good of human kind, even though we may not clearly see the way."

This passage she chose to close with the following lines:

> "I know not where His Islands lift
> Their fronded palms in air;
> I only know I cannot drift
> Beyond His love and care."[5]

This mixture of self-help and faith explains a lot about Barton's personality which would come to exude so much confidence and resilience.

The eighteen-year-old who stepped before her first class of school children in May of 1839 was uncertain about her ability to handle herself. She had far less fear that she possessed learning enough to teach the pupils what they should know. And with her tomboy years just behind her, there was no worry about what to do with unruly boys. Clara Barton had been properly raised, her mien and manner reflecting a sound upbringing. But she was far from becoming the "true woman" called for by the times and the customs. The "true woman" as perceived by society was neither aggressive, self-reliant, nor very effective. So said the preacher from the pulpit, so argued the pundit in the columns of women's magazines. And most women accepted the dictum that they be "ever timid, doubtful and clingingly dependent."[6] Clara Barton fit none of the above prescriptions, whatever appearances she may have conveyed at first sight. She was, in fact, almost the total opposite of what was called for in the "true woman," at the age of eighteen or at the age of eighty.

The state of primary education in rural New England, despite the revival of interest that had already begun to touch many larger towns, was limited to teaching the basics, but with an overarching purpose. In his essay, *On Education*, Benjamin Rush had proposed that education should "convert men into republican machines . . . to perform their part properly in the great machine of the government of the state."[7] This emphasis on civic pride and virtue to be transmitted to citizens through public education corresponded easily and naturally with the values of the Barton family. A study of American history had been stimulated by the rising spirit of nationalism following the War of 1812. For her part Clara could be counted on to present the history of her native land enthusiastically, along with the moral lessons of the Bible and the three Rs. First and foremost there must be discipline.

Insistence on discipline nonetheless had a humane aspect to it. Barton was guided in this respect by her own student experiences. The teacher, whatever his or her authority, must appear and appeal to the children as graced with human qualities. Clara's earliest teacher, Richard Stone, had made just that kind of impression, creating a strong personal relationship between himself and the earnest Miss Barton. This bond between teacher and taught became Clara's ideal, based as it was on mutual respect. Whatever the school, she sought to develop this affinity of purpose. These were some of the thoughts she referred to in the phrase "memories of a lifetime."[8]

Such rapport was not always easily attained, especially between Barton and certain of the boys she met. At her first school she was able to tame some rowdies by showing them she was as good at sports as they. Between the obedient girls and the subdued boys Clara won compliments because of her ability to maintain discipline, seemingly with a minimum of effort. When the occasion demanded, she was prepared to resort to tough measures. Her second year of teaching found her employed at a school some distance from North Oxford, one that had a reputation as a graveyard for the unwary or diffident marm. Clara was neither. Shortly after the term began she found it necessary to order a particularly disruptive student who had brazenly defied her authority to come forward to face her. Using a riding whip she tripped him and then applied the lash to his backside until he was ready to apologize to the other students as well as to her. Though she was to work in various schools over the next ten years, discipline was rarely if ever a problem thereafter.

Once she was recognized as a superior teacher Barton was much in demand. As a profession teaching required no special training so that it was easily entered upon. It was also true that as its rewards, especially in monetary terms, were meager, it was a field of endeavor just as frequently abandoned. Captain Barton's great hero, Andrew Jackson, had found it so, but their number was legion. A teacher of sterling quality was therefore eagerly sought after, on the basis of which Clara could make certain stipulations regarding working conditions. When offered one position the school board proposed to pay her less than the going rate for males. Her reply was hardly one due from a "true woman." "I may sometimes be willing to teach for nothing," she said, "but if paid at all, I shall never do a man's work for less than a man's pay."9 By insisting on equality based on ability and not gender, in ways great and small Clara showed herself a convinced feminist but not at the same time a political activist.

As serious as she was Clara was not all school and books. She was to remain unmarried but not for lack of admirers, one or more of whom might well have made a suitable husband. Her awareness of the ways of young men she had gained from her brothers and cousins. Dealings with school board officials, always males, added to her confidence when it came to men folk. There was no good reason, except by accident or by choice, why she would not one day marry. Various names of men figure in her diary, some spoken of with true affection. It is clear that Clara would set a high standard for any man who sought her hand. She could not have been happy with someone who might reveal even a trace of condescension toward women, a factor that might have narrowed her field of choice. Given the realities of her life's work, it was far more often a matter of succoring men than women, undermining any thought that she had a dislike of men or was incapable of an emotional response to them. A single state freed her to pursue her Civil War service unencumbered by husband or children. Soon thereafter Barton was totally absorbed in the fight to establish the American Red Cross. Looking backward it may not be too much to claim that Clara's compulsion to serve others left too little room for a husband. She had turned forty the year Lincoln declared the South in rebellion. Thereafter events tended to dictate the direction her life would take, even as she made everyday decisions.

Education remained the centerpiece of Clara Barton's years to womanhood. The 1840s were changing times in North Oxford in different but related ways. There was the growing awareness that an elementary schooling was the due of every child who would, it was hoped, grow up to be a productive, law-abiding citizen. A well-organized public school system, featuring proper schoolhouses, adequate supplies of basic texts, instruction by experienced and dedicated teachers—all this resting on a sound tax base—was a leading attribute of a forward-looking community. North Oxford itself had grown in size and wealth to a point where the town schools needed to undergo expansion and curriculum improvements. All this would cost money, and Clara, enlisting the aid of her brother Stephen, worked diligently to overcome the combination of indifference and hostility by men who had set their face against change. Captain Barton was, ironically, one of those who opposed the plans of his children, objectives that included a school for the boys and girls of the mill hands. After a year of persisting the Bartons, brother and sister, were finally able to bring their ideas before the town meeting. Stephen, who was later to be school superintendent in Oxford, did all the talking because Clara was, after all, only a woman, whatever her educational expertise. But her spirit helped carry the day. The town meeting agreed to revise and expand the schools, providing education for the poorest children at taxpayers' expense. Clara took great pride in the outcome even as she began to sense a feeling of stagnation. This was an understandable response for someone of her native talent and curiosity who faced the schoolhouse year after year with no prospect for intellectual stimulation and growth. Not one inclined to wait for something to happen, she decided it was time to spread her wings, to fly to a place where the lure of advancing her formal education was particularly enticing.

The options open to women to obtain a higher education in America at midcentury were strikingly limited. By 1850 only two colleges had been established that admitted women, Oberlin in Ohio in 1832 and Mount Holyoke in Massachusetts in 1839. Both these schools were thought of as experimental and very likely would have appealed to Clara Barton's native intellectual curiosity and studious habits. That she decided to attend the Clinton Liberal Institute, located in New York state, is nonetheless not surprising. The name itself proclaimed the institute as one congenial to Clara's background and outlook. Because it was not a college in the strict sense, she hoped there might be a sprinkling of older men and women, for the institute was open to both sexes, with whom she could make friends. Sponsorship by the Universalist Church heightened its appeal. And it was distant enough from home, some two hundred miles, to ensure that Clara would be able to rely on but no one except herself. No doubt she would be sorely missed by Stephen and David. Stephen especially in his capacity as superintendent of schools would feel her absence, but he never raised an objection. Both brothers warmly approved of their little sister's determination to expand her mind and demonstrate self-reliance. They understood and admired her scholarly qualities and their sense of family pride combined with love and respect to make Clara's departure from home easier for her.

The Liberal Institute proved an excellent choice. The town of Clinton was also the home of Hamilton College, and when both schools were in session a student mentality seemed to dominate. Clara had not indicated her age or her teaching experience at the time she sought admission. Once enrolled she purposely avoided making any mention of her age or that she was a veteran teacher. Petite, energetic, optimistic, her manner enabled her to keep her secret all the while she was in residence. Arriving at the end of December, 1850, she was disappointed that completion of a new classroom building was to delay the opening of the winter term. But before long she was in the academic swing. The program of studies included French and German, analytical geometry and calculus, chemistry and biology, philosophy and history and religion, all of which beckoned her. From the groaning sideboard of knowledge Clara insisted "I'll take anything they will let me take." She had a burning desire to make up for lost time.[10] The faculty encouraged Clara at every turn, for such an appetite for learning was rare among the students. The girls' principal, Louise Barker, was very supportive. A kindly woman and an educator with high ideals, she took it to be her job that every one of the students got the most of the education afforded them. Perhaps sensing that Barton was not really typical she went out of her way to help Clara settle in and then gave her her head to pursue her studies. Clara appreciated Louise Barker, recalling her as possessed of "a winning, indescribable grace which I have met in only a few persons in a whole lifetime."[11]

By building on what was a solid foundation Barton widened and deepened her book learning and knowledge of herself as a person during the nine months she was in Clinton. Because study was natural to her, though she admitted it was hard work, the time and training were immensely fulfilling even though in later years she referred to her education as being haphazard. At the urging of Miss Barker she also developed a social life. From among the young women she met, two, Mary Norton and Abby Barker, became close friends. Clara also won an admirer in Samuel Ramsay. She declined his offer of marriage, one of the true romances of her life, but Ramsay and she continued to be friends, and later met in Washington when Barton was working in the Patent Office.

If there were any shadows cast over these months in Clinton it was news from home. In May, 1851, word of Stephen's indictment for bank robbery had a shattering effect. Shocking in itself it was doubly damaging because Clara admired Stephen and his many good works. After all, he had fought the good fight for the reorganization of the Oxford public schools, a scheme that had demonstrated its worth. As with Dolly's mental breakdown, Stephen's troubles were matters Clara never alluded to, nor did she apparently ever remonstrate with him about the charges made in court. The finding of not guilty was a great relief but inwardly Clara was distressed and confused by the whole affair.

Two months later, in July, Stephen wrote: "Our excellent mother is no more . . . the last end was without struggle. . . . She often expressed great anxiety for you and she has often seen you in her dreams."[12] Again Clara was deeply affected by this second blow but with her mother buried by the time the news reached her, she decided to concentrate on her studies in Clinton while grieving for brother and mother.

The death of Mother Barton closed a chapter in the life of her last born. Returning to Oxford in the late summer Clara quickly concluded that she would not stay long. She was restless and unfocused. Her brothers were busy at their business, sister Sally was raising a family, Captain Barton well provided for by David and wife Julia. The family circle seemed not to include her within it. Were she to continue in North Oxford only two prospects were open to her: factory work that she deemed wholly unacceptable and teaching, of which in Oxford at least, she had had her fill. She must find a new situation, she was certain of that. But where was she to go, and equally a concern, how was she to manage it for she was without financial means.

Her dear friend, Mary Norton, supplied answers to each of these questions. The Norton family lived near Hightstown, New Jersey. In addition to Mary there was Charles, her brother, who had known Clara at the institute and toward whom she felt an intellectual kinship, and two other younger boys. As the whole Norton family, parents and children alike, were keen to have her as a guest, Clara accepted the invitation to come to stay for an extended period. Once in Hightstown the opportunity to teach school appeared from out of nowhere. There was a school at nearby Cedarville in need of a marm. Asked if she were interested, she replied that she was ready to try.

Teaching at Cedarville was for Barton a case of *déjà vu*. The neglected school house, lack of equipment, anxious attitude on the part of the children and, of course, the usual rowdies, were all matters Clara had dealt with before. She knew enough not to alter what had been for her a highly successful approach to effective teaching. Her first objective was always to win the respect and confidence of the boys and girls by first establishing rapport. Her aim was to make the students want to learn, enabling her, in turn, to teach them what they needed to learn. Barton was determined to take her charges beyond the basics that had been standard at Cedarville for as long as any one could remember. She included instruction in American history, always a favorite subject with her, geography and natural science. Considering that the tasks were hers alone and that children of various ages were taught as one, the happiness Clara derived from her work was yet another indication that teaching might, after all, be her true calling. It did not take long for her worth as a marm to be noticed and admired by the community because of the discipline she brought to the school as well as the knowledge she communicated to the students.

Clara was not altogether at ease with herself, however. As much as she valued the friendship of Mary Norton and appreciated the kindness of the Norton family, she missed her privacy which the numerous activities of a family not her own denied her. In important ways Clara was a private person and though she might be heard in her diary and in her letters to complain of loneliness, there were many times when she preferred her own company. Call such moods reflective or meditative, and when they took on a negative cast, depressing or destructive, she felt the need and sometimes the compulsion to indulge them. At home she could readily withdraw from the family circle without giving offense. Living with the Nortons, with a swirl of goings-on, all expected to be done *en famille*, was a different matter. As much day-to-day satisfaction as she had from work and play when she stepped back to put her affairs in perspective, she grew dissatisfied and melancholy, aware that her future was without purpose. Some part of this unhappiness can be attributed to a failed romance with one Joshua Ely. They were in regular correspondence at this time in a manner that led Clara to think of marriage. When his letters stopped she went so far as to meet with him, only to discover him unwilling to maintain their friendship. Her diary entry for a day in March, 1852, revealed her disappointment. "I contribute to the happiness of not a single object and often to the unhappiness of many, and always of my own, for I am never happy."13 Was Clara perhaps entertaining thoughts of suicide?

With the school term completed in April, Barton shook off her lethargy of spirit and resolutely announced she was leaving the Norton nest. In travels in and around Hightstown, often in the company of Charles Norton whose adulation of her was evident, Clara had taken note of near by Bordentown. Occupying a commanding site on the Delaware River and a local center of trade and commerce, its history and architecture made it attractive. And Clara quickly saw that its primary education was in a bad way. Unlike Massachusetts where public-supported education was touching more and more villages and towns, in New Jersey most education was fee-paying. Free schools were judged to be pauper schools, and those who did not attend private schools tended to remain uneducated. Cedarville had a fee-paying arrangement with students paying two dollars at the close of each term. The total raised amounted to the teacher's pay. Clara had been uncomfortable with the situation. She journeyed to Trenton, the state capital, to suggest to education authorities there was a real need for public education free of cost to the students. She told how she had seen knots of boys lounging at street corners with nothing to do. When she inquired about their schooling they explained that since they could not afford private education they had to do without. Getting no encouragement from Trenton, Barton returned to Bordentown with an "idea." Why not found a free school? It was a daring thought, daring enough to fire her spirit and throw her energy into high gear. She had to convince the Bordentown leaders, just as she and Stephen had to persuade those in North Oxford, that such a school would benefit the community. And she had to convince the youngsters not attending school to join her in the venture. At first the townspeople were skeptical. Indeed, she might not have prevailed at all save for her proposal that if Bordentown supplied a proper school building and equipped it with desks and other instructional requirements she would teach without compensation. Her purpose was not to demonstrate her personal devotion to education but the genuine advantages the town would experience by having a non-fee-paying school. She had no trick up her sleeve for wooing the children, but would rely not on tricks but on powers of persuasion. She well knew how to make learning attractive and meaningful and was, in consequence, confident the school would become a place where children would want to be. Once the building was ready and the starting date for classes widely publicized, she set off. Only a handful of boys were there to greet her, more out of curiosity than commitment. Mistress Barton invited them to follow her, and before long they were entranced by her stories as she explained the geography of the world and the history of their country. The old Barton magic had worked its wonders again. The school was soon brimming with eager students. A friend, Fanny Childs, came from Oxford to assist Clara with the teaching. Her free school idea was a complete success, and the town responded by building a fine new building to house classes, turning dream into reality. Clara was stunned then when the school board insisted that a man be appointed headmaster because they determined an enterprise that included over six hundred boys and girls was simply beyond the administrative competence of a woman, and so young a woman at that. Barton took unkindly to her denomination—it was really a demotion—as "female assistant" and was further angered to learn that J. Kirby Burnham, the head, was paid $500 while she was to receive only $250. The results were disastrous for all concerned. The teaching staff became badly divided, quarrels ensued over instructional methods, and Clara's health began to give way. By February, 1854, she and Fanny Childs had both resigned with predictable results: the Bordentown free school was in disarray. Burnham himself was dismissed at the end of the school year, and finger-pointing by the local newspaper and townspeople added to the contention.

Clara Barton's heart may have been broken by these events, but her nerve continued strong. No retreat to North Oxford this time, though she could count on being welcomed there. Stephen and she had exchanged letters about the Bordentown problems, and he reassured her that she had taken the proper and necessary course of action.[14] She surely would have had in her brother a staunch supporter for any effort in the name of education in and around North Oxford. Nonetheless, and for several good reasons, Clara along with Fanny Childs decided to go on to Washington where they proposed to find work. Two deep-seated and intertwined feelings prompted this move. Clara was unfulfilled as a result of the rejection she had experienced at Bordentown. A sense of failure made her restless, needful of taking some unplanned action, searching for something new and worthwhile that would satisfy her innate drive to achieve. There were, admittedly, other, surface explanations for relocating in the nation's capital. She had occasionally spoken of a desire to live for a while in the South because of its moderate climate and Washington in the 1850s was very much a southern town in culture as well as climate. Her long-standing interest in American history and government added to the capital's appeal. Perhaps she could find there, in government service, the sort of employment that would rest her tired vocal cords. Apparently due to the lime content in the freshly plastered walls of the new school in Bordentown, she had all but lost her voice, rendering her teaching difficult and draining. One thing seems sure, she had given up all thought of returning to the classroom. That in itself marks the year 1854 as one fraught with significance in the life of Clara Barton.

Once settled in Washington and having become familiar with the town and how to get about, Clara sought out Alexander DeWitt, the congressman from her district in Massachusetts, no doubt drawing on the political reputation of her father and a kinsman, Judge Barton. DeWitt opened a number of doors for Barton, to both the political and social worlds. Among others he introduced her to Charles Mason, head of the Patent Office. DeWitt remained supportive as long as he was in Congress but Mason emerged as her patron. An Iowan, Mason reminded Clara of the sturdy New England type, a man of integrity, of decision, and of vision. DeWitt had but to suggest to Mason that she would make a valuable worker in the Patent Office than she was offered a position as clerk-copyist. She was paid at a rate of ten cents per one hundred words copied, a task at which Clara grew remarkably skillful and from which she learned a great deal about the state of developing technology in a variety of fields. In this way the job constituted part of her continuing education, something that Barton actively pursued over the whole of her life. To boot, she earned on average about eighty dollars per month, a sum sufficient to live in modest comfort. Her carefully scripted writing style and the rigorous honesty displayed in her work soon made Clara virtually indispensable to Judge Mason. The commissioner was a relentless foe of corruption, whether it was a matter of a clerk-copyist selling patent information or simple carelessness born of intemperance. Mason relied on Clara in confidential matters that came before him, and she responded by giving him her undivided loyalty.

Clara's day began as early as 4 A.M. After a scripture reading and a prayer of thanksgiving, she dressed and then studied French. French recitation followed breakfast and then a walk of a mile to the Patent Office. She arrived at 9:00 A.M. and worked until 3:30 P.M. When permitted she would take work home. After dinner the copying was again taken up, sometimes in the company of Samuel Ramsay, her good friend from Clinton days who was in Washington to write a history of Virginia.[15]

The employment of Barton and several other female copyists at the Patent Office was by no means the standard arrangement. The federal bureaucracy, however small in size, was still a man's world. Mason was one of the few superintendents who was willing to hire women, even sparingly. He had concluded that women usually made very good copyists and were much more industrious than most of the male patronage appointees. His chief, Robert McClelland, secretary of interior, was of a different mind. By bringing pressure on Mason to dismiss his female workers, Barton's position was at risk. The interior secretary deemed it unacceptable for the two sexes to work side by side. He wrote to DeWitt: "there is such an obvious impropriety in the mixing of the sexes within the walls of a public office that I am determined to arrest the process."[16] In Barton's behalf Mason resisted this attempt to deny him his most trusted subordinate. As the controversy built up Mason, for personal reasons, resigned his office, only to resume it several months later. Clara's prospects improved immediately upon his return and for the next year and a half she was paid at an annual rate of $1,400. By the standards of the day this was a goodly sum, Mason's salary being only $3,000. Mason once again took up the war on the corrupt issuing of patents, and Clara, working closely with him, developed a nose for the rotten eggs in the basket. The consequences of her return to favor was considerable sexual harassment as she became the target of cat calls and tobacco juice. Clara Barton was working in a masculine domain, where she believed she had every right to be. It would take more than dirty looks and bad language to dislodge her. More efficient than any of her male competition, Clara knew it and the men knew it. So long as Judge Mason was conducting the business of the Patent Office she was sure her right to work would be honored.

Winds of change were blowing across the land in the mid-1850s with Washington at the vortex of this increasingly ominous storm. Being the daughter of Sarah Stone Barton, Clara had long deplored the evils of the slave system. Her students were encouraged to read *Uncle Tom's Cabin* when it first appeared in 1852. The lessons of that simply told story were evident enough: slavery was inhuman. With the majority of Americans, Barton was strongly opposed to the extension of slavery in the territories but she was not, despite her mother's word, a fiery abolitionist. With the passage of the Kansas-Nebraska Act in 1854 the issue of slavery began to intensify. The new Republican Party appealed to Clara and thousands more because of its stand against the spread of slavery westward. The Southern demand for more slave states threatened the very life of the union, or so it appeared as slave owners and abolitionists fought each other in "bleeding Kansas." A sense of crisis began to grow more acute with each passing year: The Dred Scott Decision (1857), the Lincoln-Douglas Debates (1858), John Brown's raid at Harper's Ferry (1859). Clara Barton watched the unfolding of events with consuming interest.

Barton's attraction to politics and public life and her friendship with Congressman DeWitt had often taken her to the halls of Congress. She arrived in Washington too late to hear the senatorial giants—Clay, Webster, Calhoun—but the upper house continued to be the ideal place to follow the fateful pace of crisis. She was present in 1856 when Senator Charles Sumner of her own state of Massachusetts delivered his famous "Crime Against Kansas" speech. Denouncing the slavocrats who were determined to make Kansas a slave state, he excoriated them as miscreants, "picked from the drunken spew and vomit of a sick civilization." Sumner's intention was to arouse public opinion to the dangers threatening the nation no less than to insult the slave-owning class, and he succeeded in attaining both objectives. He certainly drove his point home for Clara Barton. As she was to remark in retrospect, the American Civil War began "not at Sumter, but at Sumner."[17]

Other changes of a more personal kind but full of mischief were in the offing. Buchanan's election to the presidency in 1856 foretold a drastic shift in government patronage appointees, a change all too likely to have adverse effects for Barton. Though unable to vote she had made no secret of her support for John C. Frémont, the Republican opponent of Buchanan. At one social gathering her strongly stated views caused one of her friends to plead understanding because, he said, Clara had had too many cups of coffee. The 1856 canvass brought not only the defeat of Frémont but Alexander DeWitt was also turned out of office. With Jacob Thompson as secretary of interior, Judge Mason's days were numbered. There would be new faces all round the Patent Office, those of deserving Democrats. Barton's government service appeared to be at an end, and before the year was out she found herself heading to North Oxford, to home and family.

For the next four years Clara Barton was almost totally occupied by family matters, most of which were very worrying. If she distracted herself by continuing French classes or lessons in drawing, life was nonetheless one of suffering a loss of purpose for herself while working doggedly for others in a "perfectly fearless" fashion. In instance after instance L. N. Fowler's character analysis would be vindicated, on a grand scale and again in more immediate family affairs. Vester Vassall appeared unable to provide for sister Sally and their two children. This was especially troubling for Clara because one of the boys, Irving, had long been a favorite. At the age of sixteen he became consumptive. Aunt Clara was utterly determined that he must be made well. Accompanied by his mother and in hopes that the milder air would have a therapeutic effect, he had lived in Washington for a while when Clara was at the Patent Office. But he showed no noticeable improvement. His aunt then struck on a plan to have Sally take the boy to Minnesota where the dry, cold air was said to combat consumption. At no small expense to herself Clara traveled to Minnesota. After some time there Irving wrote that he was very unhappy and more to the point his health showed no improvement. His demands for money put considerable stress on Clara. She continued to worry about Irving's condition but recognized that he was self-indulgent and that she by her kindnesses may have helped to make him so. Add to this the case of Mattie Poor. Mattie was a young relative studying music in Boston. Barton had defrayed part of her expenses. Refusing to take a job teaching, the girl continued to badger Clara for money. Worries mounted because of a growing anxiety about Captain Barton's advancing age and declining health. He had made his home with David and his wife after the death of Sarah. When Clara came back to North Oxford she too lived with brother and father. A feeling of resentment on the part of David and Julia became more pronounced the longer Clara stayed with them.

Failure to find suitable employment added to Barton's frustration, and the deepening depression that followed. She realized even more fully than she had in Washington that her sex was against her, skilled and intelligent as she was. She was wearing herself down for the welfare of others but continued to believe her efforts went unappreciated. She longed for a *perfect* rest, expressing her discontent in such a way as to suggest suicide as an answer to her plight. In July, 1860, writing to Sally's other son, Bernard, who had joined his uncle in North Carolina, Clara uttered a *cri de coeur*: "when the command should come, Lay down thy burden and rest, it must be the sweetest hour of my whole existence . . . sometimes my stubborn heart rebels and I mourn to myself, how long, Oh Lord, how long?"[18] In this state of mind she was fortunate to be able to turn to old friends, including Fowler and the Bertram family with whom she had first stayed in Clinton. But such kindnesses were mere palliatives for a sore distressed soul. What was really missing in Clara Barton's life was a cause grand enough and worthy of her willingness to serve others in a "perfectly fearless" way.

## NOTES

1. Several biographies recount the life of Clara Barton in varying detail and in distinct but complementary fashion. These include: William E. Barton, *The Life of Clara Barton*, 2 vols., New York: AMS Press, 1969; Percy Epler, *The Life of Clara Barton*, New York: Macmillan, 1915; Elizabeth B. Pryor, *Clara Barton: Professional Angel*, Philadelphia: University of

Pennsylvania Press, 1988; Ishbel Ross, *Clara Barton: Angel of the Battlefield*, Indianapolis: Bobbs Merrill, 1949; Blanche C. Williams, *Clara Barton: Daughter of Destiny*, Philadelphia: J. P. Lippincott Company, 1941. Clara Barton has left a fragment of her life story in *The Story of My Childhood*, Meriden, Conn.: Journal Publishing Company, 1907.

2. Ross, *Angel of the Battlefield*, p. 4.

3. Clara Barton, Address to May Festival of Women's Suffrage, Clara Barton *Papers*, Library of Congress.

4. Ross, *Angel of the Battlefield*, p. 4.

5. William E. Barton, *The Life of Clara Barton*, vol. I, pp. 46–49.

6. Barbara Welter, "The Cult of True Womanhood, 1820–1860," *American Quarterly*, 18 (1966), pp. 151–174.

7. Benjamin Rush, "On Education," quoted in Russell B. Nye, *The Cultural Life of the New Nation*, New York: Harper Brothers, 1960, p. 155.

8. Clara Barton, *The Story of My Childhood*, pp. 97–98.

9. Pryor, *Professional Angel*, p. 23.

10. Manuscript sequel to *The Story of My Childhood*, Oct. 12, 1908, Clara Barton *Papers*.

11. Pryor, *Professional Angel*, p. 33.

12. Stephen Barton, Jr. to Clara Barton, July, 1851, Clara Barton *Papers*.

13. Barton, Clara Barton Journal, March 31, 1852, Clara Barton *Papers*.

14. Williams, *Daughter of Destiny*, p. 32.

15. Ibid., pp. 55–56.

16. Pryor, *Professional Angel*, p. 59.

17. Epler, *The Life of Clara Barton*, p. 27.

18. Barton to Bernard Vassall, July 28, 1860, Clara Barton *Papers*.

# —— 2 ——

# *Battlefield Commission*

The Civil War has been rightly estimated as the central event in the American historical consciousness. But a people cannot have a consciousness of something that has not yet occurred, of history yet to happen. For the generation that saw the prospect of a civil war grow larger and larger, for Clara Barton's generation, the 1850s must have appeared as an impending tragedy at once formidable and dangerous, but at the same time uncertain as to its onset, its dimension uncharted and its outcome unknown. To the very last there were many, more numerous no doubt in the North than in the South, who felt that open warfare could be averted, that still another compromise would forestall bloodshed. Barton was among the optimists. In January, 1861, she ventured the opinion that the Southern fever "was wearing itself out in its infancy and if wisely left alone will die a natural death long before its maturity."[1] And the last efforts at compromise continued to be frustrated by a lack of support in the Congress, which itself reflected a lack of trust among the states, North and South. After ten years and more of rivalry and jealousy, of accusation and counteraccusation, of failed leadership and failed partnership, the war between the states became a reality.

Viewed backward from 1861, the Civil War took on the design of ordination, what some later historians were to term "the irrepressible conflict." The forces promoting separation had overmatched the power holding the union together, a bond that had prevailed in previous crises. Men, even the most prominent, whether officials or ideologues, Northern or Southern, of good will or ill, appeared to have exhausted their options. There was nothing left to do but have it out. The American nation had succumbed to mortal battle because the Constitution no longer served the interests of the whole.

When President Lincoln called for seventy-five thousand volunteers to put down the rebellion (Captain Barton held that three-hundred thousand should have been mobilized at once) he did so in the name of the Union.[2] Secession directly challenged the survival of the government of the United States. Feelings of mutual trust and confidence, fundamental to the birth and growth of the nation, had reached a point of sterility by April of 1861. Three months after having expressed the view that the Southern fever would break, Clara Barton, fully sympathetic with the president's first wartime message, was prepared, as was Lincoln, to pick up the gauntlet thrown down by the firing on Fort Sumter. "I pray that the thing [the Union] may be tested," summed up her state of mind and spirit.[3]

Lincoln looked beyond material superiority, seeing the need of a moral principle, if the Union were to be sustained by arms. This was an imperative, vital to success, the more so should the war turn out to be of great length. From the outset the president saw through to the center of things. The Union must not be allowed to fragment; that would mean the end of the great American experiment of popular government under law. What the Founders had envisioned was a union more perfect than a confederacy. America's future, the world's last best hope, was at stake. The risks of trying to destroy the rebellion by resort to arms were formidable, yet circumstances gave Lincoln no other choice than to proceed, sending large armies against the South, by resorting to every measure possible, from suspending the writ of habeas corpus to emancipating the slaves, in order to undermine and outflank enemies both North and South, at home and abroad.

In his message to Congress in December, 1862, Lincoln addressed his fellow citizens with these thoughts. "The fiery trial through which we have passed will light us down in honor or dishonor, to the latest generation. . . . We shall nobly save, or meanly lose the last best hope of earth. In giving freedom to the slave we assure freedom to ourselves."[4] As the president moved to combine the cause of emancipation with the cause of Union Clara Barton moved with him. In the wake of the Emancipation Proclamation Barton, while in South Carolina, came to understand the plight of the freed men and women. She was solicitous for their well-being, seeing they were without education, without property. She gave them such supplies as she could spare and made time to teach a few to read, though in the overall problem facing the black population these were gestures and no more. When it came to providing care for black soldiers enlisted in the Union army, Barton stood forth as exceptional. To her they were heroes. "Whiter blood than theirs has often failed to exhibit traits as high and noble," as she was to write after witnessing how patiently the black soldier bore his wounds.[5]

Despite the appeal of the twin causes: Union and Freedom, Lincoln and Barton were to learn that many battles would be lost and won before the war was brought to a successful conclusion. The risks until the very end were high. Lincoln paid with his life; Clara Barton bore the heavy burden of devotion to "her boys." The death of the president was a stark demonstration that individuals were expendable, from private soldiers to the commander-in-chief. As for the fighting only a handful—Lee, Grant, Sherman—could claim to be indispensable. But in the caring any number of women stood forth: Dorothea Dix, Frances Gage, Mary Bickerdyke, Mary A. Livermore, Katherine Wormely, and Clara Barton. Barton has come to stand for all the women who worked to help the cause of Union and of emancipation, acknowledging the "hindrance and pain, and effort and cost" they all had endured.[6]

In the waning days of the Buchanan administration Barton had been recalled by the Patent Office. Clearly she had kept her lines of communication open in Washington. There was good reason, given the poor quality of work, to show her help was required. In the absence of Judge Mason things had deteriorated badly. If it was not quite a matter of "Clara to the rescue"—after all she would once again be a clerk-copyist at a reduced rate of pay, eight cents per 100 words—people of her skill and devotion were both remembered and needed. The sharp reduction in staff could only mean that those who were employed would have to work harder. It was a situation to Clara's liking.

More importantly, Barton was back in Washington, a capital city that, after the election of Lincoln, was rife with rumor and full of uncertainties. Lincoln remained an enigma, and if there was wholesale speculation at the probable turn of events after his inauguration, the appearance of business as usual had best be maintained. The Confederate states had already formed a government, yet it was impossible not to look forward to the new president's response to all that had happened since his election.

During these lame duck days, Clara was to make a fresh conquest in the political arena. Her cousin, Elvira Stone, was a good friend of Senator Henry Wilson, and it was she who smoothed Barton's path on the way to meet the powerful senator from Massachusetts. As he was chairman of the Military Affairs Committee she could have made no better ally. With Wilson's backing Clara believed the Patent Office job was hers to keep. She was feeling very much a part of the Washington scene. "I must confess," she wrote to her nephew Bernard, "that I fear I am getting a little dissipated, not that I drink champagne and play cards, oh, no, but I do go to levees and theatres."[7] She attended a huge party given by President Buchanan but missed Lincoln's inaugural ball because of a bad cold. However, she was in the audience when Lincoln delivered his inaugural address. His words she deemed firm of purpose but moderate as to the means to be used to bring the states back into the Union. She wrote to Annie Childs, "a more orderly crowd I never saw and general satisfaction was expressed at the trend and spirit of the Address."[8] Moderate or not, the South had already spoken.

Clara Barton's presence in Washington that fateful April of 1861 was part of her destiny. It was not planned, but it was fortuitous. Looked at soberly it could be expected that she would continue in her duties at the Patent Office while loyally supporting the Union side, exactly as most women folk would do: visiting the hospital wards, writing letters for incapacitated soldiers, making bandages, knitting socks. That she emerged as a much different kind of Civil War figure was due almost entirely to her determination to serve the soldiers in the field, to become as close to being a soldier as conditions permitted. In her own mind this was what her soldier father expected of her. As she was later to recall, "The patriot blood of my father was warm in my veins."⁹ There is indeed a tide in the affairs of men, and no less in the affairs of women, which taken at the tide leads on to fortune.

With the fall of Fort Sumter Lincoln quickly assumed the responsibilities of commander-in-chief. What was at once required were regiments from the firmly loyal nearby states of Pennsylvania, New Jersey, New York, and Massachusetts. As these units moved south several were ordered to bivouac in eastern Maryland. There secessionist sentiments ran high. Maryland must be secured to the Union at all cost. If allowed to slip away into the Confederacy, the Federal capital would be surrounded by rebel forces which could have delivered a knockout blow early on. The eastern regions of that state were so hostile that Lincoln had recourse to the use of martial law, suspending the writ of habeas corpus. Arrests of notorious pro-Southern citizens swiftly followed. For the president it came down to a matter of doing what had to be done while enduring the criticisms of those who contended that his actions were extraconstitutional if not unconstitutional.

The temper in Baltimore was so enflamed that Union troops had to fight their way through the city, as they moved from one railroad depot to another. Such was the experience of the sixth Massachusetts, volunteers from the western part of the state with many young men recruited from North Oxford. As the regiment made its way through the city streets it fell victim to mob violence. Several soldiers were killed and many more wounded, the first wartime casualties. Word of its plight had spread by the time the sixth reached Washington. The men were in need of virtually everything because they had been stripped of their baggage. Accommodations were in desperately short supply, and Clara Barton found some of the men deposited in the Senate chamber, awaiting orders.

When Barton had news of the Baltimore débâcle she immediately swung into action. These were her people, and that bond of affection only added strength to her natural resolve to be of help to those in need. She moved on several fronts. First of all there were the immediate requirements to be satisfied. Collecting clothing and food and distributing all she gathered together made her face a familiar one among her erstwhile neighbors. Boys of the sixth Massachusetts and of the fourth and eighth New Jersey regiments (drawn from the Hightstown-Bordentown areas) soon were counting on her. At the same time she chatted with those she met, talking to them in small groups, and reading from their hometown newspapers. The *Worcester Spy* in particular made for good reading material. Clara realized instinctively that an army may march on its stomach but morale was built on more than food, especially of the army kind. Clara also spread the word back home that the troops could use both necessities and pleasantries, from shirts to socks to jellies and liquor and, to her consternation at first, tobacco. She wrote her cousin Elvira Stone, "you would laugh at the sight of the half-yard slabs of plug lying at this moment on my table, waiting for Dr. Sidney's Basket of Whisky to arrive to accompany it to (Camp) Kalorama."[10] The response of Massachusetts to her pleas was overwhelming. By June Clara had to rent new quarters to accommodate the bountiful harvest of home-front generosity. These were heady days for Barton, the shadows cast by defeat were yet to descend. She was happy to be among her own again while serving far from home. In her naiveté she was longing for the battles to begin, sure to be proud of her boys in action. She did not have long to wait.[11]

During the earliest days of the Civil War the Union high command appeared to operate on two basic assumptions. One was that the sure way to victory was to capture the enemy's capital and thus destroy his ability to continue fighting. This was standard textbook lore drawn from the writings of Baron Jomini and taught at West Point as a rule of warfare. The second was even more simplistic: the shortest distance between two points being a straight line, the Union army must proceed along a line drawn from Washington to Richmond. Accordingly Federal forces marched south across Virginia and were met by

Confederate troops at Manassas Junction. What followed was the first Battle of Bull Run. After some initial success enemy resistance stiffened. What promised well ended in a rout of the Union soldiers as they ran pell-mell in the direction of Washington. Casualties were heavy and made more numerous by the paniclike retreat. The implications of all this were more sobering than the loss of a single battle, however costly. This war of brother against brother was certain to be a long and bloody one.

Barton was stunned by the outcome of Bull Run. Romantic notions of war quickly evaporated. She was no longer content to minister to the boys in camp. That could be left to more timorous souls. Clara wanted a direct part in the battle itself. She wanted to be a participant, as close to the action as possible. As the wounded struggled back to the capital, the shortage of doctors and nurses, and of medicines and stretchers was woefully apparent. Clara for the moment was thrown off balance. But she saw there was much work to do, and she doubled her efforts in aiding the wounded. Slowly she came to admit to herself that she was not doing enough, a mere witness to the suffering that engulfed her. No, she must be on the field of battle and not on the sidelines, not in the rear areas. But was this really possible for a woman? It seemed altogether unlikely that Clara Barton could go where few women had gone before. As she pondered these ambitions she continued her work at the Patent Office, somewhat irregularly it seems. But the job was necessary, it was her only regular source of income for herself and for the largesse she was always ready to shower upon the troops.

The last days of Captain Barton stiffened Clara's determination somehow to find her way to the battlefield. In the spring of 1862 she was in North Oxford as her father's life ebbed away. He had frequently urged her to become part of the fight, dismissing talk that such behavior was unbecoming a woman. "I know soldiers and they will always respect you and your errand," he told her as he lay dying. Toward the end he spoke to her, saying that Clara was "the daughter of an accepted Mason" and on that account she must "seek and comfort the afflicted everywhere."[12] The grip her father always had on Clara tightened as his body grew cold in death. He had given her a mandate. The challenge was to measure up to her father's word. She required nothing more to harden her resolve than to know that she was fulfilling his expectations of her.

The obstacles facing Barton, were she to meet and overcome the challenge, were considerable. Women simply did not go into the field. As her father was dying she wrote to Governor Andrew of Massachusetts, seeking his assistance. "If I know my own heart, I have none but right motives. I ask neither pay nor praise, simply a soldier's fare and the sanction of your Excellency to go and to do with my might whatever my hands find to do."[13] At the moment there was little Andrew could do. As he pondered Barton's request to serve with the sixth Massachusetts regiment then assigned to Burnside's division, the governor received an unsolicited letter from a Dr. Alfred Hitchcock, recently returned from the war zone. "I do not think at the present time Miss Barton had better undertake to go to Burnside's division to act as nurse," he advised.[14] Clara was stunned. The need for medical assistance had continued to increase as the war went on as was evidenced in press reports. With the war being directed from Washington, Barton knew that any chance she had to achieve her purpose was more promising once she had returned to the capital. There she was determined to seek fresh opportunities to plead her cause.

Barton's instincts were those of a free-booter, yet circumstances were not conducive to the individual initiatives she favored. The Sanitary Commission and the Christian Commission though private, volunteer agencies, nonetheless, had been accepted by the army as useful auxiliaries in the provision of supplies and assisted the army medical department in various other ways. Furthermore an order issued by the Surgeon General William Hammond required one third of the nurse corps be made up of women, the expectation being they would be assigned to hospital duty. All three of these organizations, the two commissions and the nurse corps, offered the more adventurous women an opportunity to serve the soldiers in the aftermath of battle. If Barton was to have the kind of battlefield presence she dreamed of, she would have to circumvent these agencies. Simply put,

Clara Barton was antiorganization by nature and as it developed, in a way she proved a blessing to the soldiers in the field.

The fighting in the east over the summer of 1862, from June to September, was bitter. The Peninsula Campaign, as the first phase was termed, centered on General McClellan's efforts to take Richmond from the east with Generals Lee and Jackson working to screen the Confederate capital by defeating the Union forces where fighting broke out. Included in these actions were the Seven Days battle, Cedar Mountain, and second Bull Run. Phase two, climaxed by the nearly decisive battle of Antietam, occurred in mid-September. These military engagements involved large armies, resulting in heavy casualties both killed and wounded. It was furthermore a period of great tension in the North, a time when a Union victory appeared least likely. The cost of the fighting was becoming increasingly exorbitant in the minds of many. Supplies of arms and ammunition not to mention stocks of medicine and hospital requirements were being drawn down rapidly.

It is against such a background that Clara Barton's success in gaining access to the battlefield should be read. In early July she approached Colonel Daniel Rucker, a staff member of the Quartermaster Corps. After all that branch of the army was responsible for an adequate supply of all the needs of the men in the field. Marching herself into Colonel Rucker's office, Barton, in a voice choked with emotion, cried out: "I want to go to the front."[15] Though this struck Rucker as an earnest plea his response was predictable. He explained to her that the field was extremely dangerous and therefore "no place for a woman." Besides, he added, she could little good once she got there. Not so, Clara countered. She had under her supervision a warehouse full of a variety of items the army could use, including food and medicine. She had been gathering things for months, she explained, but had been unable to persuade authorities to allow her to make deliveries. She needed to get her supplies where they would do the most good, and that was at the site of a battle. Rucker was impressed by what Barton told him and more importantly he was ready to cooperate. Not only did he provide wagons and drivers to transport what Clara had been storing, he obtained the necessary clearances from official Washington, from the military governor of the capital to the Secretary of War. Rucker had proved to be the difference between Clara Barton as one of many ladies who visited hospitals, made bandages, engaged in various auxiliary activities and Clara Barton the battlefield presence whose efforts on behalf of the wounded and dying soldiers became the stuff of legends.[16]

The Peninsula Campaign was fully under way when Barton and her wagons appeared at Fredericksburg, Virginia, in early August, 1862. Warmly greeted by the officers and men at the encampment, she was especially happy to be in the midst of the twenty-first Massachusetts. The food she had brought her wagoners quickly distributed. It must have been reassuring to her that being so close to the front, close by the enemy, she felt no cause to worry. On the contrary she was at ease, pleased to be an object of praise and thanksgiving. This calm was soon broken, and Clara was thrown into the maelstrom of bloodshed common to the shock of battle. The agony of men crying out for aid spilled over her like some all encompassing wave of horror. For the first time she was face to face with the reality of war, with death and destruction on a frightening scale.

The details of the battle may be briefly told. Union troops under General Nathaniel Banks attacked the enemy positions at Cedar Mountain. Despite being outnumbered two to one, Banks ordered his two under-strength divisions to make a frontal assault, driving back the surprised rebels. Their numbers, however, were insufficient to hold the field when subjected to a punishing counterattack. Banks suffered heavy losses, up to thirty percent of his command killed or wounded, amounting to two thousand soldiers lost. This was the moment of truth for Clara. She could cut and run out of fear or revulsion at the bloody scene, or she could stay. The thought of dying and wounded men left unattended was too much for her to bear. Convention dictated that at most she should wait until the wounded came straggling to the rear; there they could be treated. Those unable to leave the place of the fighting must take their chances with living or dying. Refusing to wait for authorization, something she was unlikely to receive, Barton decided "to break her shackles" and move onto the field.[17] Even so it was four days after the fighting had subsided before Barton, accompanied by two civilian helpers, arrived at what was to her a scene of indescribable horror, the groans of men in the throes of death agony pounding in her ears. At first she despaired in the realization that she "was only a woman."[18] Her hesitation was momentary. Stores of food and water, of medicine and bandages, all that she managed to bring forward were given away as fast as possible. The soldiers, lying helpless, were suffering from sunstroke, dehydration, and shock as well as from wounds received in the fighting. It was a matter of doing as much as could be accomplished, knowing that for many it would be too little and too late. Over the next forty-eight hours Barton drove herself relentlessly: cooking meals by improvised fires, applying dressings, assisting the surgeons—perhaps the most gruesome of tasks—and offering solace to all by soothing words and tender embraces. To hold a hand for a moment or two, to whisper words of encouragement to the suffering, to wash a wound, apply a fresh dressing, all these acts and more she undertook until she fell to sleep from exhaustion. The war in all its grim reality was now part of her experience. No one not there could imagine the extent of the carnage and the depth of the grief. Instead of being revulsed, now that she could look back on the hellish picture, she could not be content with hospital work in Washington. She was more determined than ever to claim her place in frontline duty. The cause of the Union was best supported by undertaking the most difficult tasks, that few if any others could perform; for Clara Barton it was not to be the easy road. Duty was her watchword; as it had been for Captain Barton, so it was to be for his youngest.

The heavy blow Union forces had sustained at Cedar Mountain in early August was followed by a more devastating defeat before that month was over. The buildup to the second battle of Bull Run, the battle itself, and the lingering aftershocks would cost the North sixteen thousand casualties out of an army of some sixty-five thousand effectives, or almost a quarter of the men committed. What Clara Barton had witnessed at Cedar Mountain was raised to the eighth power at second Bull Run. By September 1 the rebel armies would be at Chantilly, Virginia, a scant twenty miles from Washington. The capital was gripped with fear, confusion reigned. If the defenses of the city were formidable, the spirit there was shaky. Secretary of War Stanton appeared to sound the tocsin of alarm when he asked government clerks to leave their jobs and head out to meet and lend aid to the retreating army. The response was generous but organization was haphazard and therefore not really effective. One contingent of volunteers was drunk by the time they arrived at the collapsing front. They were frightened by it all, broke into stores of wine and brandy intended for the wounded, and lost all sense of proportion. Before long they were bribing ambulance drivers to allow them to be taken back to Washington, providing an inglorious footnote to what was otherwise a valiant effort by people such as Barton to succor the victims of defeat.

As all Washington awaited news of the outcome of the battle Clara went into action. She knew from first-hand experience that delay of even hours could mean added loss of life and continued suffering for the wounded. Her mind was full of memories of the aftermath at Cedar Mountain. This could be worse. Haste would not make waste but the very opposite, haste would prevent further waste of body and spirit. Barton turned to the Sanitary Commission, asking to draw on its stores. With permission gladly given she assembled her team of helpers, including Reverend Cornelius Welles who had assisted her before, along with three additional women. Clara was utterly convinced that women must be accorded an active role close to the fighting. She did not, however, minimize the dangers they were about to face. Worried about her personal safety, she wrote to instruct her brother, David, to look after her affairs "if anything happens to me."[19] Whether a typical woman could face the terrible slaughter might or might not be so. Barton was certainly concerned about the women in her charge. Judging by experience it took not only exceptional women but equally exceptional men to withstand the trials at hand.

Fairfax Station was the point where the wounded were being collected, a kind of halfway station between Bull Run and the hospital wards of Washington. It was a fearful place as Barton and her team discovered. Three thousand men lay in one meadow, sundrenched, the more fortunate having some straw upon which they were put down, but largely unminded until Barton arrived. At Fairfax were emergency surgeries, the doctors awash in blood and piling ever higher the mounds of amputated arms and legs as they all too often failed to save the lives of men brought to them. But for Clara this was no time to weep, or to reflect on the desolation. Instead she must be quick to act. Writing to her cousin Lizzie Shaver, in a letter dated September 4, she gave graphic descriptions of what she was able to accomplish amid the groans of despair that filled the late summer air. "The men lay so thick we could not take one step in the dark. . . . we had two water buckets and five dippers . . . hard crackers . . . my one sauce pan for making coffee. All night long we made compresses and slings and bound up and wet wounds when we could get water. . . . We took meat from our sandwiches and gave it to them and broke the bread into wine and went to feed the poor sinking wretches as they lay in the ambulances."[20] Amazing as it may seem Clara was rarely too tired to put down her feelings and her observations in her journal or letters. Informal as this writing was, it was replete with the kind of detail that conveyed a sense of the war, of the bravery of "her boys," and her ongoing dissatisfaction with the work of the army medical department. In letters and journal entries Barton showed herself an accomplished story teller and an astute reporter, public evidence of which surfaced when she embarked on a postwar lecture tour. It is not unlikely that she hoped her letters would be circulated to a wider audience than kinfolk and friends.

Two incidents occurred in the days immediately following second Bull Run that became part of the Clara Barton legend. She was already hailed by one army surgeon, Dr. James Dunn, as the "homely angel." She had appeared unexpectedly at his surgeon's tent with much-needed medicine and bandages at the very moment he had exhausted his own supply. Clara was now to become the "Angel of the Battlefield," a characterization that dying men instinctively used when she moved among them. Hearing the cries of one mortally wounded man as he pleaded for his sister, Mary, to come to his side, Clara pretended to be that sister as she cradled him in her arms. With reassuring words she rocked him to sleep, making him as comfortable as she could. Reports of this little episode spread rapidly among the troops. By this action Clara Barton had expressed the spirit and the style of her commission.

The next day as she continued to walk among the sick, feeding and soothing them, she was alerted by a Union cavalryman that the rebels were within an hour of Fairfax Station and coming on fast. He offered her a horse should it become necessary to make an escape. Clara Barton—a Confederate captive, that was unthinkable, and yet it could happen. She continued her ministry seemingly oblivious to the approaching danger, not wanting any man to go untended. At last Barton realized that she could delay no longer lest she fall into the hands of the enemy. At the last minute she jumped aboard the only train left as it pulled out of the station headed for Washington. Looking backward she sighted Confederate cavalry and the station in flames. This was indeed the stuff of legends yet unborn. Meanwhile there were the wounded to look after as the hospital train lumbered its way slowly to the capital.

The summer campaigning season in the east was by no means over as August gave way to September. The rebels having failed or unable to take advantage of their proximity to Washington to lay siege to the city, the capital was now safe. Yet the North continued to be vulnerable to attacks that might be launched farther west along the border states. Lee believed his Army of Northern Virginia had good prospects for knifing into south central Pennsylvania from jumping-off positions in Maryland, perhaps getting as far as Harrisburg. There he planned to destroy the railroad bridge across the Susquehanna River thus cutting the east off from the western sectors of the Union. Such a stroke would be especially demoralizing and no doubt would stir antiwar elements to renewed criticism of Lincoln, of his conduct of the war, and of the war itself. To be fully carried out, this plan required large numbers of Confederate troops, their movement along an east-west line hardly to be disguised for long. Clara Barton got word of this shift in Southern strategy when an army messenger, his superior officer unknown, handed her the following intelligence: "Harper's Ferry—not a minute to be lost."[21]

She knew exactly where to turn to meet this pending emergency, and Colonel Rucker did not disappoint her. He provided her with four wagons, heaped with supplies of all kinds, with army teamsters as well. Accompanied by Reverend Welles and four civilians, all men, Barton headed out of Washington for the west. There was close to a hundred miles to travel over some very rough roads, but matters of distance or comfort meant little when Barton sensed she would be needed once the battle was joined.

Harper's Ferry fell easily to Stonewall Jackson. But at nearby South Mountain there had been a fierce fire fight. Each side had inflicted heavy losses. When Barton and her band of brothers reached the site of the battle there was evidence of this all around. In Barton's own phrase, the bodies of men lay everywhere on "that field of death."[22] Pausing briefly the team gave what aid it could. But Clara guessed there was a bigger battle and a bigger slaughter ahead. The column of army wagons stretched out over ten miles, with Barton's four wagons at the tail end. This alone caused her not to tarry at South Mountain. When the wagon train rested at night Clara pushed her contingent along the road once the others had pulled over. With this maneuver she came close to the lead wagons in time to be in the best possible position once the fighting began.

The battle of Antietam was fought September 17, and in the wake of its flow of blood it may have been Clara Barton's finest hour. No description that purports to encompass the whole of her experiences during those awful hours could ever be offered. It is enough to record one or more episodes, singled out from the chaos surrounding her. One moment she was at work with her pocket knife extracting a bullet from the jaw of a young soldier, the procedure done without chloroform for the boy and with some trepidation on Barton's part. Shortly thereafter as she was giving a wounded man water to drink a bullet passed the sleeve of her dress and struck the soldier dead. She encountered her old friend, Dr. Dunn, once again and was able to provide his surgery with dressings and blankets. To which the doctor exclaimed: "The Lord has remembered us; you are here again."[23] Discovering some cornmeal among the packing crates, she mixed it with water and wine to make a hot gruel for the suffering soldiers. They savored her care quite as much as the nourishment provided them. As the night wore on Clara discovered dozens of lanterns in a nearby barn to be used to light up the areas where the surgeons were going about their grisly tasks, hacking away at arms and legs shattered beyond repair.

The battle of Antietam if not won, McClellan having allowed the badly mauled army of Robert E. Lee to make its escape, had not been lost. In the largest sense the outcome of Antietam provided President Lincoln with the occasion to issue the preliminary Emancipation Proclamation, a move that at once altered the meaning of the war. At the same time, Antietam and the Proclamation taken together finally swept aside the prospect that England might aid the Confederacy in any sustained way. But Clara could know nothing of this, or much cared perhaps. Her thoughts were elsewhere, with those she had left behind. Aching with fatigue she slept most of the hours it took for a wagon to cover the eighty miles back to Washington. Arriving at Sally's house, she collapsed in her sister's arms.

For a month Clara remained in semiseclusion, only slowly overcoming the lingering effects of the typhoid fever she had contracted during the hot and humid days of August and September. The respite was to be brief, however. By late October the Union high command was ready for another strike at Richmond, this time proceeding overland. The initial objective was Fredericksburg where on December 13 another bloody battle would be fought. Meanwhile, once her strength had returned, Barton visited hospitals where her presence and soothing words were warmly welcomed, gathered supplies against the day when, inevitably, she would be back in the field and worried, as with most of her countrymen, when the next clash of arms would take place and what its outcome would mean for the war. Despite Union successes in the west where General Grant had emerged as the man of the hour, it was commonly and correctly understood that only victory or defeat in the east would determine the fate of rebellion. Clara

Barton, of course, was ever hopeful of victory but the happenings at Fredericksburg would dampen her spirit.

Leading a wagon train provided by the Quartermaster Corps, Barton and her assistant, Reverend Welles, with more stores than they had ever before carried, had moved into the battle zone by the end of the first week of December. Such was her welcome by the officers and men that momentarily she was once again caught up in the romance of war, as at the same time she brooded over the impending destruction.

The battle of Fredericksburg, December 13, was one of the worst Union defeats of the war. Federal casualties were to number thirteen thousand in a single day. The battle plan was simple enough; execution was slow, confused, and in the end, utterly tragic. Union troops numbering over one hundred thousand assembled along the Rappahannock River at Falmouth. They were to cross the river and occupy the town. With Fredericksburg in Union hands the march to Richmond could begin. But Lee had been given time to entrench both the town and the high ground above it. As dawn broke the battle began. The Federals were under heavy fire almost from the start. At first Barton worked with her accustomed skill at points far from the fighting. But as the day wore on and more troops were able to force their way to the Confederate side of the river, a messenger from one of the army surgeons delivered the following plea: "Come to me— your place is here."[24] Defying all odds and advice she was soon on her way across one of the pontoon bridges as it was swept by hostile rifle fire. Once ashore Barton was in the midst of the battle, closer to death than at any time before or after. Exploding shells and relentless small-arms fire rent the air, a portion of her skirt torn by a piece of shrapnel as men around her were falling dead and wounded.

Late in the day General Burnside ordered a direct assault upon rebel entrenchments on Marye's Heights. At a stone wall near the summit Union dead were piled in stacks of five and six. It was a blood bath. Though fighting was over at dusk, a truce was postponed for forty-eight hours, the battlefield remaining off limits. Due to the delay and the freezing cold, men who might have been saved surely died, and those dead were frozen in grotesque caricatures, "swollen to twice their natural size." Here lay "one without a head, there another without legs, arms and legs without a trunk . . . with fragments of shells sticking, oozing from the brain, with bullet holes all over puffed bodies," ran one hellish account.[25]

Both the improvements by the army in delivering medical assistance to the front lines and the extraordinary efforts of Clara Barton and Cornelius Welles were overmatched by the firepower the soldiers faced. Clara never faltered (Walt Whitman did) in the face of the horror, but the situation was beyond her grasp. She could aid but a relatively few of the hundreds of wounded and dying men as they called for help. For two weeks she stayed on at Fredericksburg doing what she could, but it was clear that the Angel of the Battlefield had been outdueled by the Angel of Death. In the face of this Clara Barton did the supremely natural thing: she wept for the fallen.

In the larger picture of the war in the east, it was a time for the Union troops to lick their wounds. For Clara the interruption in the heavy fighting afforded her the chance to rest while at the same time resolving that her battlefield commission had not expired. But it was not the occasion to sit idly by. As always there were fresh stores to gather for by now she realized how truly essential they were to the soldiers of the line. With such work she was totally familiar. In another quite different activity she was becoming increasingly proficient. She lobbied the halls of Congress for improvements in the army ambulance and medical corps. And she wrote letters to relatives and friends back in Massachusetts, giving them accounts of her experiences, always stressing the bravery of the men at arms and the patience with which they bore their pain and suffering. To Clara they were true heroes.

Some things about the war had changed and in ways that would affect Barton directly. By the spring of 1863 the war was two years old and in that time the army had begun to learn some of the hard lessons the war had taught. There was a recognition that nothing less than an organized system of aid stations, collecting points, and field and general hospitals would meet the bloody demands of the fighting. The nursing corps was fully organized and hard at work. The Sanitary

Commission and to a lesser extent the Christian Commission and the Catholic Sisterhoods, though nongovernmental in their foundation, were integrated with the official system of medical assistance. Dorothea Dix had been named to head up the Department of Female Nurses, confirming the changes in the making. Did all this militate against a "one-woman show" that had been at the core of Barton's work? She saw the new methods without being convinced that her singular approach would be no longer accepted. But was she not becoming obsolete as the "Angel of the Battlefield?" Something akin to this would take place regarding her very own creation, the American Red Cross. That organization would grow rapidly, to the point where it became prudent to bureaucratize its management, replacing the single-proprietor mentality that had featured Barton's leadership from the start. But in 1863 Clara was determined not to allow this to happen, and at the time powerful friends in conjunction with the circumstances of war combined with her own force of character to enable her to continue as a battlefield presence.

In May of 1863 Barton accompanied her brother David to Hilton Head, South Carolina. David Barton, a civilian at heart, had been commissioned a captain in the Quartermaster Corps due to the influence of Senator Wilson. These duties took him to Hilton Head, at the time a remote and rather quiet sector of Union military operations in the east. But headquarters had some big plans. From the Sea Islands Union commanders planned to attack Fort Sumter and Charleston counting quite as much on psychological as military victories. Charleston was a bone sticking in the Northern throat. For such an undertaking large amounts of supplies would be called for, absolutely essential to Union success. Additional quartermaster personnel had to be on the scene and David Barton was among them. The War Department had cleared Clara to attend her brother. Given the battle plans this was to be no idle jaunt for Clara who thought herself fortunate to be arriving on the very afternoon when the heavy guns were to be brought to bear on the fort and the city. To Clara, Charleston was the seed-bed of rebellion and deserved to feel the power of Union guns. On paper the Union plan was simple enough, both logical and sound; execution was another matter. The assault was a failure, much to the chagrin of the commanders who promptly drew back and settled for a blockade of the city.

What promised to be an active if secondary theater of operations for Clara turned into an interlude of easy living. She confessed to feelings of guilt to Mary Norton. "I only wish I could work to some purpose. I have no right to these easy, comfortable days and our poor men suffering and dying. My lot is too easy and I am sorry for it."[26] Despite misgivings Clara enjoyed being the object of attention on the part of some of the officers stationed there. In the officers' mess the tables were laid with silver and linen, and the food some of the best Clara had ever tasted. With little else to do, as the siege wore on, Clara took to riding horseback daily. She also had plenty of time to read and write letters and, alas, to brood over her inactivity. After all, "up North," some of the great battles of the whole war were being fought, including Chancellorsville and Gettysburg, and Clara Barton was to have no part in them.

Two personal considerations kept Clara at Hilton Head whatever her qualms of conscience. Her brother found it awkward dealing with the military, and he grew progressively more lonely and morose the longer he was away from wife and family. Clara's continued presence at Hilton Head meant much to him and to her, convinced as she was that he needed her close by. David's melancholy aside, Clara preferred to stay on because of her attraction to Colonel John Elwell. Elwell was at once handsome, intelligent, well read, witty, a person of lofty ideals and most important, equally attracted to Clara. What grew between them was a love affair, one of those brief, compelling, incandescent relationships that wars in all ages have had a way of fostering. Burning fiercely it dies as the moment passes, as circumstances change, in this case, the anticipated arrival of Mrs. Elwell.

It must have been a release for Clara that General Quincy Gillmore, the commanding officer, frustrated by his failure at Sumter and Charleston, was once again ready to undertake offensive action. This time he planned to storm Fort Wagner, located at some distance away on Morris Island. Barton was to accompany the expedition, prepared to lend assistance to any battle casualties. After a heavy bombardment Union infantry went ashore and almost at once became bogged down in the wet sand surrounding the fort. What developed was nothing less than a turkey shoot for the Confederate riflemen. From one of the Union vessels Clara watched with horror as more than one-third, about fifteen hundred men, went down before enemy fire. Colonel Elwell was among the wounded.

What especially appealed to Barton was the presence of the fifty-fourth Massachusetts regiment in the attack formations. This unit was composed of black soldiers under the command of Colonel Robert Gould Shaw. With the capture of the Sea Islands abolitionists, many from Massachusetts, had launched the Port Royal experiment, designed to show that liberated bondsmen would display a work ethic appropriate to a free people. In turn, the battle performance of the fifty-fourth Massachusetts would demonstrate that black men could prove themselves worthy members of a citizen army. All this held great meaning for Clara.

Barton was immediately back in action. She waded ashore despite the danger and ministered to the men as they lay bleeding or worse. Her style was intensely personal: the kind word, the cool drink, the tourniquet tightened, the brow softly stroked. She was equally ready to attend the surgeons, once a primitive surgery had been set up. She also found herself alongside Frances Gage who had come to the Sea Islands to help in the practical matter of making freedom a reality to the ex-bonds-people. As the two women worked side by side they gained a mutual admiration and respect. Barton was rarely at ease when she was not alone but such was Gage's spirit and ability that Clara was disarmed. They became close friends in 1863 and remained so for many years thereafter. Eventually Fort Wagner fell, reduced to a pile of rubble. Barton and Gage stayed on to look after soldiers who now became sick from rancid food and dirty water. As it was impossible to bury the dead in the shifting sand or to evacuate so many bodies the place gave off the smell of death.

Barton's best efforts did not gain the full approval from General Gillmore on down. Complaints about army inefficiency which she frequently voiced openly and her requests to draw stores from the quartermaster, where her brother was prepared to accommodate her, earned further resentment. Friction between the invited guest and the official hosts was inevitable. Put simply, the army did not appreciate a freewheeling civilian, and a woman at that, in their midst. Clara was ordered evacuated from Morris Island, and shortly thereafter received this terse communication from Gillmore.

The Brig. Gen. Commanding is informed by the Medical Officer in Charge of the hospital on this island that your services will no longer be required in connection with the hospital in the field, as the sick and wounded are not to be retained here but will be sent immediately to Beaufort. I am instructed to say that the General appreciates the value of your kind offices to the sick and wounded soldiers, and the benevolence which has led you to sacrifice so many comforts by residing here in the actual zone of conflict, but in view of the crowded condition of the island and the many inconveniences which such a residence must entail, he deems it best that you should remove to Beaufort, where he will provide for you a comfortable dwelling.[27]

For Barton this was a repudiation of all that she had done and all she stood for. In truth the message was less harsh than Barton chose to interpret it. There was praise in the general's words as well as ingratitude. But to Clara any show of displeasure was intolerable. For the moment it seemed like the end of the world. But she had an uncanny resiliency enabling her to bounce back. As in past periods of stress her depression was deep but short lived. Frances Gage, with her special brand of encouragement, was the best medicine Clara could have had.

It is a mistake to confine Clara Barton's Civil War endeavors and outlook to the field, not denying that in the heat of battle she achieved her greatest sense of accomplishment and satisfaction. There were larger concerns however. She never lost sight of what the war was all about, namely the preservation of the Constitution and the Union. Whether it was incompetent generals, greedy contractors, or overbearing bureaucrats she was loud in her denunciation of those she considered timeservers, or worse. Because she had the ear and the sympathy of Senator Wilson she was in a much stronger position than the average citizen to bring pressure to bear on people she deemed malefactors. A letter to Wilson, dated April 14, 1864, is a good example of her determination to root out the unworthy. "Is there no right? Are there no consequences attending wrong?" she cried out. "Shall lies prevail forevermore? . . . The pompous air with which little dishonest pimps lord it over their betters. Contractors ruining the nation and oppressing the poor and no one rebukes them. I doubt the justice of almost all I see."[28] In other words, why could not all people serve the cause of the nation devoid of selfish, wrongful ambition.

Evidence of interests wider than aiding battered soldiery would, of course, surface long after the war was over. Her advocacy of the American Red Cross and its early history with Clara at its head were consistent with this and an expansion of her wartime career. Similarly her support of the cause of feminism was further proof of the range of her convictions about the place of women in a modern society. It is simply that the war forced her to focus on the well-being of the battle casualties. Once the war was over Barton would seek and discover fresh outlets for her love of country and of mankind.

Adding to her distress over repudiation by General Gillmore, a matter that was a virtual humiliation for Barton, more personal matters also intruded to make her weary. News of the death of Reverend Welles was a blow, complaints about her absenteeism from the Patent Office she deemed the height of ingratitude, considering how she spent her time away from a desk. Concern over David who remained at Hilton Head when she returned to Washington persisted. The success of Dorothea Dix in making the Department of Nursing integral to the army medical service was unsettling. Worry piled upon worry. Frances Gage stayed in South Carolina, leaving Clara dangerously alone. Thoughts of suicide came from deep within her as a diary entry for April 19 clearly showed. "I can not raise my spirits. The old temptation to go from the world. I think it will come to that some day."[29] If only for the moment Clara Barton was a troubled soul.

A new and more deadly turn in the fortunes of war caused Clara to throw off her mood of self-occupation and return to the field. In

1864 campaigning in the eastern theater of operations was under the command of General Grant. His strategy was to be the very opposite to that of McClellan. Grant proposed to engage the enemy as frequently and as heavily as possible. Only in this way could the Confederate armies be defeated, and only in this way could the Union prevail. Richmond as a military objective became largely irrelevant. Lee's army was now the prime target. Grant's pressure tactics sought to wear down his opponent, trading if necessary two Union lives for every Confederate life. The price Grant was willing to pay was to prove staggering, and as the "butcher's bill" grew in size the nation, and even many of the most ardent Unionists, were scandalized by the slaughter. Such was the extent of casualties ensuing from this style of warfare that the army could not afford to turn aside any offers of assistance. With all her heart and soul Clara Barton felt the call.

By May, 1864, Barton was at Fredericksburg once again, arriving shortly after the fight at Spotsylvania Court House, where death again took a holiday. In a letter of May 16 she gave voice to her anguish at the scenes she witnessed. "For the first time in the history of war the magnitude and intensity of the suffering and want is so appalling as to wring from me a public call for aid."[30] Even the elements appeared to be in a conspiracy against compassion. The heavy rains were steady, turning roads into quagmires. It became impossible to evacuate the wounded by ambulance as the wagons settled a foot deep in the mud and could not be budged by man or mule. By the hundreds the wounded were squeezed into the premises of the only hotel in town, placed so close together they could be barely tended to. Barton moved among them as best she could but found the refuge a wakeful nightmare. What particularly infuriated her was that dozens of homes in Fredericksburg, untouched by the fighting, had been placed off limits by Union officers. They considered the men too dirty, too bloodied to be admitted to a suitable place to lie, and in all too many cases to die. Barton thought this off-limits order unconscionable, virtually treasonous. She made a hurried trip to Washington and placed her findings before Senator Wilson. Such was his faith in Clara's judgment he went at once to the War Department and put officers on notice that if the army failed to act to correct conditions in Fredericksburg senatorial investigators would be on the spot the next day. Wilson had made his position clear, and within hours many of the finest homes in town were occupied by the sick and wounded soldiers of the Army of the Potomac. Clara took great satisfaction for her part in making right a grievous wrong.[31]

Spotsylvania was quickly followed by another major battle at Cold Harbor. Again the casualties were awesome, again the hospitals were filled, and the surgeons at their gruesome tasks. And again Clara was in the midst of the chaos. Feeding, touching, smiling, even singing in attempting to keep up morale, no one now doubted that she was once more an angel of mercy. Among those who were quick to acknowledge this was General Benjamin Butler, a Massachusetts man and a friend of Henry Wilson. The senator had given Clara a letter of introduction to Butler. The two hit it off immediately. Butler, belying his reputation as a "beast," was gracious and kind. More importantly for Clara he was eager to make use of her skills by putting her in charge of nursing at one of the field hospitals under his command. Upon investigation it was obvious that someone was badly needed to take responsibility for nursing and diet, and Clara agreed to accept the general's invitation. From the start she was determined that every man in her charge would be properly fed rather than be asked to subsist on crackers and coffee, the food she had often been reduced to serving to soldiers in the field. Being in charge of the diet meant simply that Barton became the cook, and that she had always been good at. Her daily routine went something like this. "I have had a barrel of applesauce made today and given out every bit of it with my own hands. I have cooked ten dozen eggs, made cracker toast, corn starch blanc mange, milk punch, arrowroot, washed hands and faces, put ice on hot heads, mustard on cold feet, written six soldiers' letters home, stood beside three death beds . . . now at the hour of midnight I am too sleepy and stupid to write a totally readable scrap. It has been a long day, and mercury is at something over a hundred and no breeze."[32] And the next day and the day after would be much the same.

The kind of hospital Clara was supervising was often termed a "flying hospital" due to its frequent moves forward as the fighting developed. To be as close to the action as possible without risking being run over by the enemy was the ideal arrangement for looking after those of the wounded requiring immediate attention. This entailed the most critical kind of assistance but Clara was no longer the lone figure walking among the dying. She had become an administrator involved with numerous details necessary in running the hospital. Even at that as long as Barton was the one and only nurse the work suited her. When the staff was enlarged she was less comfortable. Dealing with others, men or women, in any but an authority capacity did not come easily. Problems arising from this flaw in her character would trouble Barton throughout her career. Too often she took suggestions for criticism and critics easily became enemies in her sight. When working with less forceful individuals than herself she tended to prevail, but when she encountered those of strong character the results could be a standoff or retreat, a situation that could produce depression.

For all her devotion to her soldier boys, her own family was never very far from Clara's mind. In the autumn of 1864 her great concern was Stephen Barton. He had been arrested by Union troopers who were uncertain whether he was a Confederate or a Northern man turned traitor. After confiscating his possessions, including over a thousand dollars in cash, money he used in his business transactions, he was lodged in a military jail in Norfolk. Stephen Barton had been in an awkward position from the start of the war. Obviously Northern and a recent arrival in North Carolina he tried to maintain both his neutrality and his property after 1861. With the instincts and daring of a shrewd businessman, he traded cotton for badly needed medicine, earning significant profits from these dealings. Not quite legal from the Confederate point of view he was nevertheless allowed to carry on his activities. To the Union, however, his business amounted to a violation of the blockade, a serious offense. While languishing in jail Stephen managed to smuggle out a letter which came to Clara in a roundabout way. She appealed at once to General Butler "to do something." He took a personal interest in the matter, out of admira-

tion and respect for Clara. Stephen was ordered released from prison
and brought to the hospital Clara was supervising. There she would
try to bring him back to health. This would not be easy. Only
fifty-nine years of age, in his prime Stephen had been a strapping man.
Now he was a wasted figure, malnourished, feeble, and broken in
spirit. Eventually acquitted by a military court martial of all charges
against him, his property in Carolina was lost forever. When he was
strong enough to make the trip, Clara took him with her to Washington where Sally, Stephen, and she could be together. But Clara did not
intend to stay in the capital, only to discover that Butler had been
relieved of his command. This signaled the end of her association with
the flying hospital. Stephen lingered only a while, dying in early
March. His sister took his body home to be buried in North Oxford.
Stephen's odyssey had been a strange one.

The death of the long-suffering Irving Vassall occurred a scant two
weeks later, another loss that Clara could bear only by calling upon
reserves of fortitude. Somewhat self-centered as a youth, Irving had
worked in Washington for the Massachusetts state relief agency
throughout most of the war, and his aunt was very proud of him for
that. Finally in April came the political murder of President Lincoln.
In victory death seemed to dominate. As for her own future that was
very much in doubt.

Barton had no desire to return to live in North Oxford, no interest
in returning to school teaching, and disillusioned by the attitude of
workers at the Patent Office, she was unwilling to renew that kind of
government service. Suitably she found a worthwhile cause in the
aftermath of the war: missing persons. As hostilities wound down
more and more stragglers found their way north, arriving for the most
part in Washington, or if they came by sea, at Annapolis, Maryland.
They needed help in getting back to their units, or more likely to their
homes and families. It was a sobering but uplifting challenge, a search
for missing men and as it turned out, a search for grave-sites. Once
Barton became well aware of the difficulties faced by these wartime
castoffs she went to Senator Wilson with a plan to meet their needs.
Could the administration be persuaded to establish some sort of

missing soldiers bureau, with Barton in charge? As always she offered her service in the spirit of personal sacrifice, seeking no compensation. Though she was never to meet the president to plead her purpose, Wilson put the plan to Lincoln and after some delay Clara received this communication over the president's signature.

> To the friends of Missing Persons:
> Miss Clara Barton has kindly offered
> to search for missing prisoners of war.
> Please address her at Annapolis, giving
> her name, regiment, and company of any
> missing prisoners.
>                            Signed
>                            A. Lincoln[33]

President Lincoln's laconic announcement of Clara Barton's new responsibilities was dated March 11, 1865. By that time any number of Union soldiers who had been prisoners of war or who had been separated from their units for one reason or another had made their way north, with Annapolis becoming an unofficial center for these refugees. Barton took up her station there, prepared to pursue objectives that were both humanitarian and practical in nature. She felt deeply the anguish of loved ones not knowing the whereabouts or, as it would prove in thousands of cases, the fate of the missing men. The soldiers she met in Annapolis were often disoriented and in need of advice and direction. Again she was expected, virtually by herself, to bring some semblance of order out of the chaos created by soldiers arriving in a constant stream. The army was not sure how it should proceed. Barton as a free agent found it easier to take initiatives that might begin to break the log jam which was fast building up. With an eye to moving quickly, Clara was ready to draw on her own private resources rather than wait for official funds to be available. She had been accustomed to operating on the margin. What she had done in wartime, procuring supplies with her own money, she was equally willing to do now that there was a new and worthy cause to serve.

With Lincoln's announcement more and more widely disseminated it was not long before the tide of incoming mail reached flood stage in Annapolis. Letters by the thousands came into the Office of Correspondence with Friends of the Missing Men of the United States Army, as her undertaking was termed. In light of the size of the task, one half of the Union dead had never been identified and perhaps as many as two hundred thousand had been placed in unmarked graves, a less dynamic spirit than Clara might well have faltered. To accomplish the impossible she recruited a loyal band, perhaps no more than a dozen helpers, including sister Sally, Samuel Ramsay, her friend and admirer from Clinton days, and Jules Golay, a young Swiss who had volunteered for the Union army. He first met Clara when he had been hospitalized for wounds received in battle. Barton to be sure remained the organizing force behind these men and women but their support was crucial in what she was able to accomplish.

Barton's method of operation was simple enough. When an inquiry was received the name of the missing soldier was listed according to his state. Lists were then circulated to local newspapers, displayed in post offices, and reviewed by various fraternal organizations. The hope was that veterans seeing a particular name might recall the fate of one or more of those cited, communicate that information to Barton who would in turn write her findings to the person who had made the inquiry. To facilitate this enterprise the army was prepared to offer stationery and a franking privilege but little else, at least at first. Later a large tent and some chairs and tables became available. But it was from beginning to end a shoestring operation.

The inevitable result was a cascade of responses to the published lists, providing information both reliable and unreliable. Each response had to be coupled with the letter of initial inquiry and the information transmitted to the family of the missing person. All this amounted to a paper chase of considerable dimension. Good intentions, even when combined with total dedication, were insufficient to meet the heavy demands placed on Barton and her team. Perhaps no more than fifteen thousand of the missing men were reported on by the Office of Correspondence. This was a fraction of the total number of missing for which a report was appropriate, which would have been welcomed by caring and grieving relatives. The important consideration to bear in mind is that Clara Barton was the first to step into the breach, ahead of the army's efforts to account for the missing. She was in consequence able to take great satisfaction from knowing that she had laid many ghosts to rest, that she had helped the widow and the orphan come to terms with the death of loved ones.

In all likelihood Barton's endeavors would have been confined to receiving and answering letters save for an offer of assistance by Dorence Atwater. Atwater's story was a remarkable one in itself and his offer to help Barton enabled her to make a further contribution to burying the dead. Atwater was an eighteen-year-old soldier in a New York regiment when taken prisoner near Hagerstown, Maryland, in July, 1863. After being detained at various Confederate prisons he was sent to Andersonville, located in a remote part of Georgia, arriving there in February of the next year. Placed in the infamous stockade he soon fell ill and after some recovery was assigned to the Surgeon General of the Confederate army. His job was to record the death of each prisoner, by name and by date. With men dying at a rate of one hundred a day Atwater found this a wearing task. He decided, nonetheless, that he would make his own copy of the death list. Upon his release from Andersonville he carried his list hidden in his belongings and without the knowledge of authorities, Union or Confederate. His purpose was entirely patriotic, he wanted to be sure that the nation would know what happened at Andersonville. His list contained fourteen thousand names, written in a neat script. Once he had come north and though still a soldier on active duty, he approached military authorities seeking some compensation for his efforts. Specifically, he asked the sum of $300 and a position in the War Department as a civilian employee. He did not offer to sell the list, viewing it as his personal property, proposing only to allow the army to copy the names.

Aware of Clara Barton's good offices in the matter of missing prisoners Dorence Atwater contacted her and told his story. After several unsuccessful attempts Barton was able to inform the secretary of war of the situation at Andersonville as Atwater had described it. Secretary Stanton was eager to have the graves properly marked and that a soldiers' cemetery be constructed on the site of the former camp. It was intended as a fitting tribute to those who had died at the hands of their Confederate jailers, and a means of keeping the spirit of hostility alive in the victorious North.

A large party was assembled, consisting of some forty workmen who would build the cemetery and as needed bury or rebury the dead. Captain James Moore was the officer in command, and both Barton and Atwater were invited to make the journey south. The expedition arrived in Savannah, Georgia, in early July. After that the journey became arduous as there were few roads and inadequate transport. Moore was ready to call off the enterprise at one point, until direct orders from Washington required him to proceed. Barton's prodding of Moore and her annoyance that the trip was taking so long exacerbated a bad relationship between them. Moore apparently resented Barton's presence both as a civilian and as a woman. In this clash of personalities not surprisingly Clara more than held her own.

Andersonville deserved the notorious reputation it had gained during the war, one that it has retained in history. At any one time it might hold twenty-five thousand Union captives. Built on a treeless plain and lacking shelter for men half clothed and malnourished the death of many was certain. Clara had met and talked with survivors of the camp, and they had impressed her as men who had suffered from a deliberately cruel treatment. Now in late July she saw the deserted camp; it gave mute testimony to the brutality practiced there on those she considered "her boys." Her reaction was one of pain and bitterness.

Because records had been carefully kept and Atwater had a remarkable memory for the location of the grave sites, it became a relatively easy matter to place name markers at each burial place. Meanwhile the carpenters and laborers were hard at it, laying out walks, building fences, and landscaping the grounds. They worked with a will at their macabre task, not wishing to linger any longer than was required. On August 17 a dedication ceremony took place. Barton was asked to raise the flag of the United States. "I ran it up midst the cheers of the builders. The men stuck up the *Star Spangled Banner* and I covered my face and wept," was part of her diary entry for that day.[34]

The days spent at Andersonville, barely a month, had nonetheless given Clara time to reflect on the war and what it had come to mean to her. Affection for the freed men and women now became more spontaneous and more natural. She realized that legislators and their laws would not be enough to secure the reality of freedom, much less equality, for the former bondspeople in a predominantly white society. Barton promised herself that she would be ever mindful of the burden the black Americans would have to carry, and she would strive to make that burden lighter whenever she could. Conversely, the images of suffering soldiers evoked by Andersonville left her angry toward the South and the rebellion it had spawned and at what terrible cost. She readily embraced the sentiments expressed by Senator Sumner, that the proud traitors must be humbled, that the Southern states be treated as conquered provinces. Finally as she left the tragic scene for a return to Washington, she was more than ever aware she was a figure of some prominence, her name known and her war service admired. This consideration would prompt her to want to use her influence in good causes, great and small.

Identifying the missing and learning of their fate was a task far from completed by the autumn of 1865. With funds rapidly being depleted Barton decided to petition Congress for an appropriation, both by way of recompense of money already spent and in anticipation of future needs. A sum of $15,000 was approved by Congress, with some critics questioning why she should be paid at all. She had been a volunteer, as were many others who supported the war effort. To recompense Barton was to set a dangerous precedent. Clara did not see it that way at all. At Christmas time she was to refuse the offering of twenty dollars by Senator Wilson. She was embarrassed; the senator owed her nothing. A grant from the government was a different matter. The government, in her judgment, owed her a great deal. She had after all expended her own funds to the point that she was at times close to want. The sum received from Congress was a token rather than full payment for the debts she had incurred. Should this attitude be thought of as sullying Clara Barton's reputation, does it make her sacrifice any less praiseworthy? For all her emotional involvement in the cause for which the Civil War was fought, Barton was an extremely practical, no-nonsense individual. She had made a request for money only at the point beyond which the good work she was involved with could no longer be carried forward. To Barton that seemed a reasonable expectation. Had she not been awarded the funds it is altogether likely that she would have continued, somehow, to do the labor she would require of herself. It was a lesson she had learned as a youngster: leave no chore unfinished.

Poor Atwater! His association with Barton cost him dear. The army continued to demand that he surrender his copy of the list of the dead at Andersonville. Upon refusal he was arrested and his living quarters searched, but no list was found. He had given it to Barton. She kept her silence, at Atwater's request, aware that he was to be court martialed. He was found guilty of insubordination, fined $300, and given a dishonorable discharge. In addition Atwater was sentenced to eighteen months in prison. Clara made a strenuous effort to obtain his release, without success. Luckily he was freed after two months, on the strength of a general amnesty declared by President Johnson.

Barton persisted in her desire to have the list published in full by someone other than the army which she continued to believe had treated her unkindly because of her difficulties with Captain Moore. She approached the flamboyant editor of the *New York Tribune*, Horace Greeley. He agreed to publish at his own expense a seventy-four page pamphlet, listing the names of the missing soldiers. Meanwhile letters continued to arrive at the Office of Missing Men in decreasing volume. As the mail lessened so Clara's spirit lowered to the level of depression. Once again she faced a familiar question: what shall I do now?, for action was the essence of her life.

Joseph Sheldon first broached a possible answer but Frances Gage was more convincing. On a visit to Clara after the New Year, 1866, she followed up on the advice she had written her some weeks before. She had urged Barton to join the lecture circuit, and now she renewed her encouragement. Gage reminded Clara that her war experiences, if not unique, were nonetheless worth telling, that her account of happenings was bound to be of interest to thousands, perhaps especially to women. "You can lecture. Tell the world as you told me of the sufferings of our brave boys in blue."[35] It was good advice, and it conformed with Barton's own desire to keep the memory of Civil War sacrifices in the public consciousness. Lecturing had the added advantage in that it would provide much needed income. Barton would be able not only to meet living expenses, she could earn enough to enable her to continue the Office of Correspondence on a reduced scale. Lecturing, beginning in the autumn of 1866, went on until late 1868. Once Barton reached the decision to go on tour she spent months in preparation, both in research and writing. She drew together several distinct yet similar talks, with such titles as "Work and Incidents of War," "How the Republic Was Saved, or War Without the Tinsel," and "Scenes on the Battlefield." All the lectures were well rehearsed, yet she was able to convey a sense of freshness and spontaneity that made her quite literally a spellbinder. Not that Clara was ever at ease on the podium. Stage fright was a regular occurrence that she managed to mask by sheer force of will.

In planning the tours Barton employed an agent and she was booked from Adrian, Michigan, to Yonkers, New York, not quite A to Z. She entranced audiences with her recall of details of days in the field. There was little need for her to embellish; she simply told it as it was. Her fees averaged from seventy-five dollars to one-hundred dollars but as she wrote to a sponsoring group in Akron, Ohio, if the fifty cents admission was deemed too much it should be reduced accordingly. Barton was not speaking primarily to make money, but to tell her story. Dorence Atwater accompanied Clara as a secretary-companion, Clara treating him almost as a son, and he made himself indispensable because of the wide-ranging travel involved.

Were these talks nothing more than a sentimental binge for both speaker and audience? It would have been impossible and hardly understandable deliberately to avoid stirring emotions and even passions. The war had been a savage one, and the civilian population was well aware of that. In large measure Clara brought home to her listeners the reality of war, in so far as that can be conveyed by the most vivid of stories. Of all the famous lecturers of the day, only she had seen action in the war. This gave her a special authority and lent added credence to what she said. Her accounts were definitely partisan, the Southern side of the struggle was of little interest to the people of the east and midwest. No doubt Barton sounded her own trumpet, doing so in a fashion that revealed her courage and dedication rather than showing her as self-serving. The egocentric predicament Clara disposed of truly and well. On occasion she used her lectures to settle old scores, as when she related the plight of the well-meaning Atwater. She also offered some general criticism exposing the inefficiency of the army and the slack attitude of some of its officers. These were the only occasions when the audiences were not with her. But Clara would be heard.

In the long run this two-year stint of lecturing was a master stroke of good fortune. In the event she became a national figure winning respect and admiration in all parts of the states that composed the victorious Union. She had hardly planned it that way, but thereafter she was willing to trade on it. It is difficult to believe that she would have been able years later to persuade a president and a Senate to embrace membership in the International Red Cross, except for the legend of Clara Barton, the Angel of the Battlefield, the American Florence Nightingale. It was a legend she herself had enhanced by means of her lectures. If she symbolized the sacrifices of a host of women who had brought aid and comfort to wounded and dying men, she also capitalized her own fame.

The indomitable Clara did have a breaking point, however. Toward the end of 1868, scheduled to give a talk in Portland, Maine, she was unable to go on. She was suffering from near total exhaustion. When she attempted to begin the lecture the words would not come. She had no choice but to cancel her remaining engagements. Returning to Washington a sick woman, she decided to wrap up the work of the Office of Correspondence, and submitted a formal account of its accomplishments to Congress. Although the office had identified only ten percent of the men the army declared missing, Clara Barton, by having a leading role in undertaking the correspondence, had provided singular assistance to many families of the war dead.

Barton's wartime experiences proved to be the shaping event of her life. What exactly had the war done to require her to rethink her purpose for the years ahead, and how to pursue it successfully? In December, 1868, Clara celebrated her forty-seventh birthday, not an advanced age but given the life expectancy in the United States at the time, she was getting on in years. But Clara Barton was forty-seven years young, young in mind and young in spirit. Her future plans were bound to be influenced by her ordeals and her triumphs. In the first instance what she had learned from Sarah Stone Barton, namely, women must be treated as equals to men, caused her to stand for the advancement of women in all respects. Barton's post-Civil War career demonstrated as well as proved the innate equality of men and women, an abstract proposition empirically confirmed. The war had provided a singular opportunity for female assertion and a corresponding demand placed on society to accept the contribution women had made and would make to the betterment of the country, were they allowed to do so. Women's rights became for Barton an oft-repeated refrain.

The war also reinforced her respect for the innate dignity of all people, irrespective of race or color. Experiences with recently freed ex-slaves during her stay in South Carolina joined in her memory with the bravery black soldiers had displayed in some hard fighting placed Negro rights on the same level as woman's rights. In the practical order Barton opposed the effort on the part of some feminists to compromise the main purpose of the Fifteenth Amendment, designed to protect voting rights of the freedmen. Barton insisted that justice to the black man should take precedence (in practice but not in theory) over female enfranchisement. "I am willing," she wrote, "to stand back and see the old scared slave clank his broken fetters through before me—while I stand with head uncovered—thanking God for the release."[36] The war had enlisted Clara Barton in the ranks of two great reforms: woman's rights and Negro rights; at the same time her overall concern was to help all suffering men and women.

Finally there is the paradox of Clara Barton in wartime acting as both fighter and pacifist. There can hardly be any doubt that she wanted to be a soldier and came as close to being one as conventions would allow. Yet she never enlisted to kill, the mission of the soldier of the line, but to save, to heal, to comfort, and whenever possible to bring peace to those who suffered unto death. The argument derived from the conventions of the time stated that unable to bear arms she nonetheless had to be as close to the front as the situation permitted, relating to the soldiers as she had grown to relate to men in various circumstances, that is, positively and without being self-conscious. The argument from gender is different. The person that Clara Barton was as she went about her work on or near the battlefield, could only have been carried on by a woman. She became a mother-sister-daughter figure to those of the opposite sex. Only men could have visualized her as "Angel of the Battlefield," as only a woman could have performed the labors of loving care. If it is paradoxical to argue in this vein, it is part of the larger paradox of the Civil War itself. The war proposed to destroy the power of the rebel states so that they might be forced back in the Union on a basis of freedom and equality with the states that had made war on the South. As Lincoln had said from the beginning the Constitution and the Union must be preserved. The restoration of the United States was to demonstrate that Lincoln, in a feat of wartime leadership rarely equaled, was vindicated. Like the president, Clara Barton had been a true believer in the Constitution and the Union.

## NOTES

1. Barton to Elvira Stone, Jan. 21, 1861, Clara Barton *Papers*, Library of Congress.
2. Blanche C. Williams, *Clara Barton: Daughter of Destiny*, Philadelphia: J. P. Lippincott Company, 1941, p. 62.
3. Barton to Elvira Stone, April 14, 1861, Clara Barton *Papers*.
4. Abraham Lincoln, "Message to Congress, Dec., 1861," Roy P. Basler, *Abraham Lincoln: His Speeches and Writings*, Cleveland and New York: World Publishing Company, 1946, p. 688.

5. Barton to Drs. Brown and Drier, March 13, 1864, Clara Barton *Papers*; Stephen B. Oates, *A Woman of Valor: Clara Barton and the Civil War*, New York: The Free Press, 1994, p. 256.

6. Elizabeth B. Pryor, *Clara Barton: Professional Angel*, Philadelphia: University of Pennsylvania Press, 1988, p. 101; Ishbel Ross, *Clara Barton: Angel of the Battlefield*, Indianapolis: Bobbs Merrill, 1949, p. 27.

7. Ross, *Angel of the Battlefield*, p. 27.

8. Barton to Annie Childs, March 5, 1861, William E. Barton, *The Life of Clara Barton*, vol. I, p. 105.

9. Percy Epler, *The Life of Clara Barton*, New York: Macmillan, 1915, p. 32.

10. Ross, *Angel of the Battlefield*, p. 30.

11. Oates, *A Woman of Valor*, is a full account of Barton's service.

12. Ibid., p. 41.

13. Williams, *Daughter of Destiny*, p. 70.

14. Oates, *A Woman of Valor*, p. 42.

15. Pryor, *Professional Angel*, p. 87.

16. Oates, *A Woman of Valor*, pp. 51–52.

17. Barton, "Work and Incidents of Army Life," Clara Barton *Papers*.

18. William E. Barton, *The Life of Clara Barton*, vol. I, p. 129.

19. Barton to David and Sally Barton, Aug. 13, 1862, Clara Barton *Papers*.

20. Williams, *Daughter of Destiny*, pp. 74–75.

21. Oates, *A Woman of Valor*, p. 78.

22. Barton, "Work and Incidents of Army Life," Clara Barton *Papers*.

23. Ibid.

24. Pryor, *Professional Angel*, p. 106.

25. James M. McPherson, *Battle Cry of Freedom*, New York: Oxford University Press, 1988, p. 574.

26. Barton to Mary Norton, July 3, 1863, Pryor, *Professional Angel*, p. 113.

27. Oates, *A Woman of Valor*, p. 187.

28. Williams, *Daughter of Destiny*, p. 95.

29. Barton Journal, April 19, 1884, Clara Barton *Papers*.

30. Williams, *Daughter of Destiny*, p. 99.

31. Oates, *A Woman of Valor*, pp. 237–38.

32. Williams, *Daughter of Destiny*, p. 101.

33. Ross, *Angel of the Battlefield*, p. 86.
34. Barton Journal, Aug. 17, 1865, Clara Barton *Papers.*
35. Pryor, *Professional Angel*, p. 146.
36. Ibid., p. 153.

# — 3 —

# *Travels and Travail*

When in the late summer of 1869 Clara Barton took ship for the Old World, leaving her native land for the first time. She was going to places known to her but in song and story. She had little if any knowledge of conditions then obtaining in Europe, conditions that were to belie her peaceful expectations. The world of the nineteenth century was dominated by the leading European powers, with neoimperialism soon to be in full swing. At the same time relations of the various Continental nations at home were coming under increasing strain. If Great Britain enjoyed a splendid isolation, aloof for the most part from growing national rivalries, France and the German states were facing each other with a fear and hostility that were of one piece. Long the European kingpin before and after the rise and fall of Napoleon Bonaparte, French hegemony was about to be challenged by the German states that themselves were seeking to overcome a centuries-long delay in unification. German nationalism, aroused by Napoleonic invasion and Napoleonic defeat, had nonetheless been elusive. Only by mid-nineteenth century had Prussia begun to emerge as the single German state likely to provide the leadership required to transform the Germanies into a German nation. By victory in the Seven Weeks War of 1866 Prussia swept aside Austrian pretensions to a commanding place in German affairs. Four years later Prussia with the support of several other princedoms used the Franco-Prussian War as the means of crystallizing unity. Victory in that war brought the German people together in what history would term the second Reich, the German Empire. This war was to catch Clara Barton in its toils, the war and a fledgling organization, the Red Cross.

The Red Cross was less than ten years old at the time of the Franco-Prussian conflict. It had grown out of the experiences and the vision of Jean Henri Dunant. A native of Geneva, he was a successful banker and industrialist. By the merest coincidence he was witness to the battle of Solferino in 1869. Solferino was part of the Italian struggle for political unity, the *Risorgimento*. Led by Sardinia-Piedmont, the Italian states sought to oust Austria from northern Italy. France joined in this effort, partly out of sympathy for Young Italy, and partly because it wanted to extend its influence to that part of Europe. Fought on Italian soil, Solferino was a ferocious battle, with forty thousand casualties. Dunant described it as "the most murderous blood bath of the century." Into this boiling cauldron of war he stepped, volunteering personally to assist the wounded and dying. However lonely a figure Dunant must have appeared as he went among the afflicted, his imagination was sparked despite his shattered nerves. It took him some time to recover his mental balance but unable to forget what he had seen and heard he wrote *Un Souvenir de Solferino*, an overpowering account of the carnage. It left an indelible mark on thousands of readers. Another Genevan, Gustave Moynier, moved by Dunant's plea to reduce wartime suffering, formed a committee composed of both medical doctors and army officers. Before long the committee, with Moynier and Dunant at the helm, was hard at work on plans for an international conference. One of the medical people was Dr. Louis Appia who during the battle of Solferino was busy helping to save lives at a hospital close by the killing fields. Appia was later to introduce Clara Barton to the background and principles of the Red Cross.

Sixteen countries sent delegates to the international gathering in Geneva in 1864. Here the Geneva Convention for the Amelioration of the Condition of the Wounded and Sick Armies in the Field was adopted, signed by twelve nations. The Convention provided for neutrality of personnel of the medical services of the armed forces, the humane treatment of the wounded and those taken prisoner, and the neutrality of civilian volunteers offering assistance. The symbol of the new foundation was to be a red cross on a field of white, reversing the colors of the flag of Switzerland. The Franco-Prussian War would constitute the first test for the new relief organization and as it transpired, a fresh challenge to Clara Barton.

Barton was a sick woman when she left the lecture circuit at the end of 1868. Accumulated fatigue that had been building since the start of her wartime service and the demands she placed on herself as she told the country about her feats and fears were reason enough to account for her condition. Added to these considerations was what by now had become a recurring, obsessive worry: what next to do with her life.

She had been ordered by her physician to take a complete rest, nothing else would do. This was nearly unthinkable for Clara, and highly impractical. She was too well known and too much admired to be left to herself. Unless, of course, she was prepared to travel abroad. As a stranger in strange lands she could well go unnoticed. True, Barton would be carrying letters of introduction to American diplomats in London, Paris, and Geneva; but between frequent moves incidental to travel and especially in non-English-speaking countries she might be rescued from her fame. Picasso once remarked that fame was the castigation by God of genius. For Clara fame also seemed to be an obstacle to good health.[1]

Barton did not look forward to the ocean voyage itself because of the sea sickness she knew she would suffer. Even her coastwise travel during the Civil War made her violently ill. Nor did she care for the prospect of crossing the Atlantic alone. Finally, Sally agreed to accompany her as far as the British Isles, but not farther. Their ship, the *Caledonia*, landed in Glasgow after a journey of fourteen days, very trying ones for Clara. With a week in Scotland and time in London only "to see the sights," Sally was homeward bound, leaving Clara on her own. From London she proceeded to Paris, again for a brief stay, and then to Geneva where she was a guest of the Golays, the parents of Jules. She made good friends of the American consul, C. H. Upton and his wife who showed their distinguished countrywoman every kindness.

During these delightful Geneva days Clara was introduced to Dr. Appia. Her war work in America was apparently known in Switzerland and commented on favorably by the doctor. Because of his awareness of Barton's accomplishments he said he made it a point to meet "The American Nightingale," a comparison Barton was not keen on. Once the pleasantries of this first encounter were out of the way, Dr. Appia came directly to his purpose: Why had not the United States signed the Treaty of Geneva, establishing the Red Cross? Ignorant of the treaty Barton had to inquire politely about its nature. Stunned by this admission Appia offered to bring pertinent books and documents so that she might study them at her leisure. And he took the opportunity to give his own gripping account of Henri Dunant at Solferino, of support given by Moynier and others, and of his part in the movement. Once she read the literature Clara was convinced that the United States had been derelict in not joining so worthwhile a body of nations. What she thought she might be able to do about this lapse on the part of her government she could only wonder.[2]

As Appia explained, the United States had sent a representative to the Geneva conference, Charles S. F. Bowles, a member of the Sanitary Commission. He was not present as a delegate but as an observer. Before coming to Europe Bowles had discussed the upcoming meeting with Secretary of State William H. Seward. Such was the preoccupation of the Lincoln Administration with the prosecution of the war in combination with the American tradition of nonentangling alliances or commitments with foreign states that the time was simply not propitious for the United States to become a signatory. Barton could certainly understand that, recalling how all absorbing the war had become by 1864. What Dr. Appia had done, nevertheless, was to open the mind of Clara Barton to the possibility that one day her country might join the other civilized nations in this humanitarian undertaking.

By mid-December the wind and cold of Geneva were chilling Barton to the bone. In a tone of desperation she asked Mrs. Upton: "Where can I go to get warm?"[3] Rejecting a suggestion made by the consul's wife that she go to Algeria, she decided on Corsica. The promise of warm weather was not to be realized. Rooms with a southern exposure were hard to book either in hotels or pensiones. Indeed Clara thought most of the accommodations cold and ill-kept. Her adventures were not those of a celebrity. On one occasion she barely escaped a robbery with all her important papers and her money at risk, on another, the victim of an insect infestation. Throughout her time in Corsica, Clara was snubbed by hotel guests, finding the British tourist, and of these the women, consistently rude to her. A great interest in Napoleon and his birthplace that had been one of the reasons she chose to go to Corsica initially she more than satisfied in a short time. By March, 1870 Barton was again in Geneva. All in all Clara's travels had not been unlike those of many tourists.

In Geneva Barton was briefly with the Golays, only to have the Uptons insist that she stay with them. The chance to speak English would have been sufficient reason to accept this invitation but she had a genuine fondness for her American hosts, and they for her. For someone as compulsive as Clara, all was not sweetness and light however. There was little for her to *do* in fact and doing things, even misguided travel, was critical to her for keeping her mental balance. She felt she could never repay the Uptons for their many kindnesses and that troubled her. Sounding a peculiarly Marxian note she confided in her journal that she wanted to take her place "among the workers of the world."[4] By taking an interest in the activities of the Society of Orphans and Poor Schools as well as aiding several individuals in distress she calmed her nerves to some extent. And she was extremely pleased that authorities sought her out to discuss problems of Swiss emigration to the United States. Such attention was flattering. Indeed, wherever Barton went in Geneva she met admiration and respect which, given her need to sense appreciation, helped to make life less than totally empty. And yet her mood was often despondent, writing at the time that it was "just as well to live and die across the sea as anywhere."[5] Such thoughts ran counter to her often expressed love of her native land and suggest the desperation of the moment.

It is not far-fetched to say that Clara Barton welcomed the Franco-Prussian War when it broke out in July, 1870. The war was largely the enterprise of the Prussian aristocrat, Count Otto von Bismarck. As president of the Ministry of the North German Confederation which had Prussia as its centerpiece Bismarck conducted its affairs of state. He was at once astute and ruthless and well deserved his reputation as a man of blood and iron. As has been noted, for the Germans the war was a struggle for leadership in Europe and an opportunity to unite the German people under a single ruler and within a single nation. By editing the so-called "Ems Dispatch" in a way that altered its intention and stirred France, he provoked an edgy Louis Napoleon into declaring war. It was a war the Germans prosecuted with a swift and terrible sword. France was thoroughly beaten, the French emperor captured, the nation humiliated. The cost in lives was very great.

If Bismarck was an ogre to many, Clara Barton saw him in an altogether different light. She met with him personally in December because he had given some attention to her relief work. She described him as a "Tall, thin man with a kind face, and seems to be genial. He is gentle and good at heart, I think."[6] Such an estimate was unusual for contemporaries to make of a man known as the Iron Chancellor but Clara had reason to think well of him. As it happened he had provided her with another war, and she would leap at the chance to be a part of it, either through the Red Cross or by her own initiatives. Only in this way was her despondency put to a temporary and as it turned out a sporadic rest.

Barton's first thought was to volunteer her services. Surely a person with her wartime experience would be in demand, and the service she could provide would be obvious to those in charge of relief operations. No amount of advice from friend or official could persuade her to stay in Geneva. "I *Must* go," summed up her response to nay-sayers.[7] Within a fortnight she was on her way to Basle to meet with Red Cross authorities there. She was greatly impressed by the huge warehouses stocked with supplies beyond anything she had seen or the army had been able to assemble during the Civil War. But she was unable to get permission to go into the field. Being in the field, "at the front," was the essence of service for Barton. Her enthusiasm which had been so keen, was now dampened but not extinguished. It took the intercession of Gustave Moynier to "break her shackles" this time. Before she set off, Moynier suggested that she have as her traveling companion a young Swiss woman, Antoinette Margot. Margot was a Red Cross volunteer known to Moynier who worried about a lone woman going into the war zone. The two made an exceptional team, Antoinette at twenty-seven was full of idealism, and Clara nearing fifty was in need of a loyal and useful companion.

The two women left Basle together early in August, believing they were bound for the front. On the road they encountered refugees streaming from embattled towns, fearful of the pursuing Prussians, and clogging their escape. Clara's excitement mounted as she anticipated being back in the thick of things. Reaching Mulhausen, they were informed there was no need for them there. The American Consul thought it extremely unwise for the women to go any farther and suggested, instead, they board an omnibus crowded with refugees and guide these unfortunate men and women to a safe area away from the fighting. It was hardly the kind of assignment Barton had anticipated but as she liked to be "in charge," she was willing to see to it that the refugees were taken out of harm's way.

The area in which Clara and her companion found themselves was one of great confusion. Between the French and German troops roaming the countryside and fighting breaking out when they clashed, with wagons loaded with civilians attempting to get out of the way of danger there was very little concrete that Barton and her helper could do. When they stopped they were met with suspicion; for all the locals knew they might be spies. The Red Cross armbands meant nothing either to the people or the rank-and-file soldiery. What the diplomats had done at Geneva in 1864 had not filtered down to the fighting men. The hostility and suspicion Barton and Margot faced could become life threatening. Mistaken for a bar maid when they stopped at an inn Clara was accosted by a drunken German soldier. He pinned her to the wall with his sword when she refused to serve him drink. That she was not injured or killed was a matter of Barton bravado as she faced the brute down, and a heavy dose of good luck.[8] Their wanderings made no sense, and they had done nothing to ameliorate the suffering of sick or wounded, military or civilian. But prospects were soon to brighten.

If Count von Bismarck had given Clara a war, Louise Grand Duchess of Baden was about to become her patron. Baden was one of the German states in league with Prussia, and it was the Badisch army that would force the surrender of the proud old French city of Strasbourg. Both the Duke and Duchess of Baden were greatly taken with the purposes of the Red Cross, and Louise had learned something of Clara Barton's Civil War story. Having returned to Basle after her fruitless wandering over the month of August, Clara was in receipt of a telegram from the Grand Duchess, requesting her presence at the ducal palace in Karlsruhe. After some delay, a contrivance on Clara's part lest she appear too eager, the two women met in mid-September. They liked each other at once and became life-long friends. Initially drawn together by the common cause in which they believed, as symbolized by the Red Cross, they came to see much in each other to admire. Clara was shown every courtesy during that first stay in Karlsruhe. She was eager to exploit the developing friendship, requesting that she be given the opportunity to assist in the treatment of wounded Badisch soldiers. For the moment the Grand Duchess put off Barton's proposal, encouraging her instead to visit the military hospitals in the area. These left her with a dim impression: "not so good, dirt and discord" as she was to note in her journal.[9] Hospitals had always symbolized rear areas to her. She still pined to go into the field, but that was not to be.

Meanwhile Strasbourg had fallen to the Duke of Baden. A city that had been battered and beaten must surely require every kind of relief service, thought Clara. The Duke was prepared to allow her to come to survey the needs. And there was need everywhere, of every kind. Aided by the American Consul Clara was able to visit all parts of the city and desperation was written on the faces of the people as she spoke to them. In addition to the military and civilian casualties of battle men, women, and children faced starvation and the threat of plague, typhoid, and small pox. Not used to seeing women in hospitals in such large numbers, Clara was more determined than ever to relieve the suffering. She must report all that she had seen and heard to Grand Duchess Louise who, she was certain, would take immediate action in behalf of the afflicted. Of the people Barton had come to know only the Grand Duchess had the stature and influence to effect relief. Supplies were soon flowing across the Rhine to the shattered city and Clara, assisted by Hannah Zimmerman, another convert, as well as Margot, set up a center for the distribution of food and clothing. Now, Clara felt, she was engaged in a humanitarian effort, the kind of work that gave her the greatest satisfaction, other than attending the wounded soldier. With conditions as they were, she was not destined to become once more an angel of the battlefield, a consideration that seemed to count for less and less the more people were benefited.

Gradually and reluctantly Barton had come to understand that she would not be in the field. Official resistance combined with the early defeat of France to make that dream impossible to realize. At the same time, pondering their desperate straits, she was determined to do something substantial for the populace in Strasbourg. Crops could not be quickly grown to supply the daily bread but perhaps clothing could be quickly made. The idea was not clothing for the people but clothing by and for the people. Barton proposed to the Committee of Safety, the ruling body of the city at the time, that premises be rented and materials be purchased so that some of the women could be set the task of sewing garments. Clara was prepared to provide some seed money, funds she could ill afford to spend, in order to launch the venture. Failing to persuade the town leaders of the value of such an undertaking, she turned to the Grand Duchess who was eager to help.

The plan was based on the triple concept of self-help, petit capitalism, and home industry. Women were to come to a distribution center to pick up the wool and cotton cloth. Returning to their homes they would sew such wearing apparel as directed, bringing the finished product back to the center. After careful inspection to ensure the quality of the work done they were paid two francs a day. The workers would then pick up a fresh supply of raw material for the following week's work. Clara and her assistants supervised the distribution of the clothing to the poorer parts of the city as well as to nearby villages.

Barton had taken what was a good idea on paper and turned it into a successful self-help industry-charity. Her great worry was to locate sufficient funding to acquire the goods and pay the two francs per day. Her personal funds were limited and she gladly turned to others for help, the Grand Duchess among them. She even made a personal request to Bismarck. He turned down her request despite the well-reasoned argument that funds coming from a conqueror might make the Strasbourgeoise more amenable to a German occupation. Clara also directly appealed to American friends but few responded; Strasbourg seemed such a far away place. Eventually the Committee of Safety incorporated Barton's scheme with other relief activities and in this way some public funding became available. Starting with a handful of workers upwards of three hundred women became involved in the enterprise, and that had proved enough to persuade the town fathers that Clara's proposal was both imaginative and practical. By the end of 1870 Barton's name was widely known and honored in Strasbourg. A beautifully decorated Christmas tree, brought to her lodgings one evening, spoke the gratitude of the many simple people she had helped to clothe. It would be another six months before Clara would leave Strasbourg and her clothing venture. By then other trouble spots beckoned, chief among them Paris.

Paris was a tragic city during and after hostilities. As difficult as life had been for the Strasbourgeoise, the municipal government continued to function and a sense of order was preserved. For Parisians conditions were much worse. The city was placed under siege by victorious German troops, the central government of Louis Napoleon overthrown. After the surrender of Paris in January, 1871, the communards, an extremist group advocating sweeping revolutionary changes in government and society, controlled the capital for some months. Anarchy spread as food grew short and executions went forward at an alarming rate. Bringing any kind of ordered relief was virtually impossible, however worthwhile intentions might be. In addition Paris was a huge city compared with Strasbourg or Metz which had also been under siege and where Barton had worked briefly to assist in relief operations. In Paris size alone tended to compound the miseries of the populace.

All these were reasons why Barton felt she must go to Paris; the challenge was there. Accompanied by Dorence Atwater, an always faithful follower and a man to boot, no small consideration given conditions, Clara did not arrive empty-handed. She was able to arrange to load a train with large amounts of clothing, some forty thousand pieces, as well as other goods. She also carried with her some money for distribution. The situation was such that the train had to stop short of the city and Clara undertook the last seven miles on foot before reaching one of the gates of Paris. What greeted her was not a pretty sight: "I saw Paris when the Commune fell and the army of Versailles shot down its victims in the street," her words a sober commentary of the agonies of the city.[10]

Clara quickly arranged quarters for Atwater and herself and they set about to distribute their considerable store of supplies. Yet the sheer magnitude of the problems they faced discouraged them. By singling out special groups, including Alsatians, who came to the capital as refugees fleeing the Germans and the families of ships' crews, significant help was tendered to some of the dispossessed. There were other discouragements for relief workers such as Barton. The Red Cross was neither widely known nor much respected. "Artful dodgers," Paris style, were clever in directing aid into their own hands, for resale to the unfortunate. In the end the relief effort in Paris proved too much for Clara: over the summer she spent less time in aiding the poor and more socializing with the Americans living in the city. Her old Civil War contact, Eli Washburne, was United States ambassador to France. He was solicitous about her welfare and a source of invitations to all kinds of gatherings.

This relatively short time among the French of the capital convinced Clara that she had more in common with the Germans and liked them better. "Germany is much like us. There is a fixedness of purpose in her people, her anchor goes to the bottom. France swings in the water, and changes with every whipping wind."11 It must be remembered that Clara had been treated royally by Grand Duchess Louise and her relations with Bismarck were cordial. In defeated France she found no such courtesy but she seemed unwilling to take the plight of the French into her judgments. Also to the point, the Duke and Duchess of Baden were supportive of the principles of the Red Cross, an organization Barton admired as kindred to her past endeavors and perhaps part of future plans.

At the end of the summer significant amounts of American money were being sent to a French Relief Fund. The donors believed Clara Barton was in the best position to insure that the monies would be fairly distributed. Dorr Atwater went to London to act as her agent because the financial transactions were being routed through the American legation there. Meanwhile Barton had left Paris for Lyons where she met the parents of Antoinette Margot. They expressed their concern that their daughter wanted to continue to assist "the American lady." Nonetheless Antoinette was to stay by Clara's side. Barton also encountered her dear friend, Senator Henry Wilson who was visiting France in the wake of the war. The senator's visit had a wonderfully uplifting effect on Clara for they were genuinely fond of one another and he had much to tell her about happenings back home.

Receipt of funds from America made it incumbent upon Barton that she funnel them into a new relief effort. But for reasons of personal health she seemed to falter. Clara was nearly worn out. Still opportunity and means matched the needs of various towns that had suffered severely during the war, including Besançon, Belfort, and Montebeliard. Handing out money was disagreeable. To Clara it was the worst form of charity, and she was reminded of the old saying: give a man a fish and he will eat for a day, teach him how to fish and he will eat for a lifetime. Hand-outs of petty cash to one and all were, however, virtually dictated by her possession of the funds she was conscience bound to give away. She managed to get small consolation from that consideration. In fact it appears that not all the money received from America was distributed by the time she decided to return to Strasbourg in the late autumn. The city was the site of her only real triumph and the seamstresses were a great consolation to Clara. Why not give them a party? The affair that took place the last day of 1871 was a huge success. Three hundred women attended. The spirit of the Christmas holiday added to the occasion. Two great fir trees were decorated with lighted candles and many ornaments. Small amounts of money put in pouches were given to each of the seamstresses. With great satisfaction Clara recalled how her army of workers had turned out from twelve to fifteen hundred garments a week, the very model of what a charity should be. The party "was to be the highwater mark" of Clara's sojourn in the Old World.[12]

From January, 1872, to October, 1873, at which time Barton at last returned to the United States, she was to see much more of old Europe. In consequence she formed a number of opinions about the places she visited and the people she met. A good bit of her time was again taken up with travel, tourist style, and that despite ailing health. Moods of depression, as before born of what she considered a want of purpose in her life, were relieved by the kindness of friends, people such as Abby and Joseph Sheldon who were good enough to come over from London to look after her. But instead of going back to London with them as first proposed she was persuaded by other friends, Joseph Holmes and his wife, to accompany them to Italy. Milan, Pisa, Florence, Belagio, Rome, and Mount Vesuvius were all part of the itinerary, distracting Clara more than exciting her. But she did climb Mount Vesuvius and was quite proud of herself for doing it. Stopping briefly in Paris on her way north she then crossed over to London where she proposed to settle. London interested her and she did a great deal of wandering about. Among the people she met was L. N. Fowler, whom she had last seen in New York before the Civil War. His advice to Clara's mother long ago had set her on the road to accomplishment. There was London society to enjoy, if and when she felt up to it; very often she did not. The English weather she thought particularly irksome, the succession of gloomy days adding to her malaise.

Residence in London provided an ideal opportunity for Clara Barton and Florence Nightingale to meet. They had much in common and such an encounter might well have been memorable. If they did not meet it was likely due to having too much in common by way of personality and temperament: two strong wills and near superegos. Only a chance occurrence could have brought them together. Writing in 1901 Clara put a better face on their failure to see each other. "Friendly messages have always passed between us but we have never met."[13] What is more interesting is what is not said in such a passage.

In June, 1872, London hosted an international congress on Prison Reform. Among the delegates from the United States was Julia Ward Howe. Barton was eager to talk with the author of "The Battle Hymn of the Republic," that stirring expression of the highest ideals of the Union cause during the Civil War. Howe for her part invited Barton to serve on one of the committees of the congress. Good reformer that she was she was aware of the need for improving prison conditions. Beyond that she judged her countrywomen at the congress a disappointing crew. Barton concluded, probably unjustly, "they have no confidence in their success and fear a failure."[14] Two quite different conclusions are possible to draw from Clara's negative appraisal. One is that, not being in charge, she had difficulty motivating herself to get involved. A second reading is less harsh. Others had their work to do, and Clara had hers, and they did not mix well.

Barton could not indefinitely postpone going home. The original purpose of her odyssey, her health, had long been forgotten and neglected, leaving her weaker than at any previous time in her life. Yet all summer long she hesitated to make a move. She still brooded over what she considered the less than proper gratitude on the part of the government for her wartime sacrifices, occasionally expressing disinterest in going back to America. But her New England roots ran too deeply and her patriotism was too persuasive to permit her to stay in exile. In March she had learned that Sally had fallen ill, sick with stomach cancer. She kept her constantly on her mind and knew she should be at her side to nurse her back to health or to await her death. By summer's end Sally's condition had worsened and that decided Clara. She must be with her sister; family had always counted much with her. She boarded the *Parthia* for the two-week ordeal at sea, less fearful perhaps of seasickness because of her myriad ailments and Sally's pending end.

As the days at sea passed, it is evident there was much on Clara's mind. In a poem composed as the *Parthia* plowed its way westward the old question, the great question, was once more on her lips. The poem spoke her mind in its title, "Have Ye Room?" and in two clear passages:

> But if only once more I might tread the loved land,
> And toil for its weal with my heart, and my hand:
> Have ye a place, each beloved one, a place in your prayer,
> Have ye **work**, my brave countrymen, work for me there?

This theme is repeated in the last two lines of the poem, with a different emphasis.

> Have ye place, each beloved one, a place in your prayers,
> Have ye **room**, my dear countrymen, room for me there?[15]

What possessed Clara as she thought out these lines? Possibly, maybe probably, American adherence to the Geneva Convention. She had a genuine affinity for its principles and purposes, but would America view it in the same way, and commit itself to the Red Cross? To those who heard the poem, or read it soon thereafter, it must have sounded a far more personal note. Hers was the cry of a heroine without a cause.

The appeal of the Red Cross which was to become the driving force of Clara Barton's later years was but one of the legacies of her stay abroad. Europe had taught her other lessons as well. She was deeply disturbed by what she witnessed and what she heard about the treatment of women, especially in the lower orders of society. Women could be seen used as draught animals, day laborers, victims of neglect and abuse by their husbands. Barton was disturbed and she was angry. She would not soon forget such ill-treatment, believing, rightly or wrongly, that women of the poor were better off in America. Years away from home had confirmed her as a feminist. In contrast she continued to find it difficult to get along with others and her experience, however minimal, as a committee member at the congress on prison reform pointed this up. As the feminist movement went forward on several fronts in late-nineteenth-century America Barton readily identified with it, yet in large part remained aloof from its exertions. She would expect others to respect her proprietary leadership of the American Red Cross; she was equally willing to allow other women, whether Dix, Addams, or Stanton to command their followers without second guessing from her. Finally these years in Europe gave Clara a special sense of the marvel and the promise of her native land. America with all its faults! The greeting which she received in New York upon her arrival was a welcome from the heart, banishing lingering doubts about her reputation among her countrymen and women. Clara Barton was home and realized at once it was where she belonged.

## NOTES

1. See for example, Clara Barton, *The Red Cross: A History of This Remarkable Movement*, Washington, D.C.: Privately printed, 1872.

2. Elizabeth B. Pryor, *Clara Barton: Professional Angel*, Philadelphia: University of Pennsylvania Press, 1988, pp. 155–56.

3. Blanche C. Williams, *Clara Barton: Daughter of Destiny*, Philadelphia: J. P. Lippinoctt Company, 1941, p. 149.

4. Barton Journal, July 10, 1870, Clara Barton *Papers*, Library of Congress.

5. Williams, *Daughter of Destiny*, p. 166.

6. Ibid., p. 180.

7. Ibid., p. 167.

8. For a more detailed account, Ross, *Angel of the Battlefield*, p. 112.

9. Barton Journal, Sept. 21, 1870, Clara Barton *Papers*.

10. Epler, *Life of Clara Barton*, p. 165.

11. Ross, *Angel of the Battlefield*, p. 117.

12. Pryor, *Professional Angel*, p. 171.

13. Ross, *Angel of the Battlefield*, p. 171.

14. Williams, *Daughter of Destiny*, p. 207.

15. The poem is quoted in full in Barton, *Life of Clara Barton*, vol. 2, pp. 85–87.

# — 4 —

## A New Beginning

Clara's weakened physical condition made it appear unlikely that there would be a new beginning in her life. It might have been expected that once back in the United States she would continue to enjoy the respect and admiration of the nation as she quietly slipped into retirement, the heroine of two continents. Looked at from the outside there was much to encourage such a prospect. Come December Barton would be fifty-three years old; presumably her great work was behind her. Financially comfortably off she would probably choose to live in Washington where she knew virtually everyone worth knowing, right up to the vice president, former Senator Henry Wilson. Of course Clara would continue with good works, both corporal and spiritual according to her own lights, but her great days had passed. Or so it all seemed. Barton's supreme achievement, the establishment and direction of the American Red Cross lay short years ahead. Not even Clara, for all her indomitable will, could have predicted that her service to mankind would stretch into the next century. On the other hand, that very indomitability was to make such a thing happen.

How could this be? First of all she must regain her health, both her physical stamina and her mental balance. There were problems of a psychosomatic kind. If as the medical doctors who attended her insisted, there was nothing organically amiss, why should she be crippled to the point of incapacity by a weakened condition. The death of dearest Sally in May, 1874, had an almost paralyzing effect. She had seen Sally immediately upon her return from Europe but after some weeks of visiting kinfolk in and around North Oxford had retreated to what she deemed a better climate for her health, the capital city. By the time she had mustered the strength to go north again Sally had died and Clara blamed herself for failing to see her sister one last time. She lay stricken, unable to read or write, unable even to stand unassisted. This condition did not last long but there was no denying her frailty. The death of Henry Wilson in November of the following year dealt another blow. Glories of past achievements, symbolized by the Iron Cross given by the Kaiser, the Gold Medal of Remembrance presented by the Duke and Duchess of Baden, the Red Cross awarded by the Queen of Serbia, honors she had rejoiced in and would do so again, these were mere baubles in her bereaved state of mind.

What was the nature of her undoubted illness? William Barton has stated it in the simplest and perhaps most meaningful terms. He described her as possessing "a temperament abnormally sensitive . . . capable of enduring almost any physical or nervous strain . . . [but] when the strain was over and she met some trivial exhibition of ingratitude, some capricious and wholly negligible criticism, some petulant despicable bit of opposition, her nervous system gave way in a sudden collapse. Her Voice failed; her eyes failed; whatever organ was weakest gave way first."[1] Clara was burdened with such a weight of vanity, totally out of proportion, that she became at times dysfunctional. Such a thought she might not entertain but this much must be admitted, in matters pertaining to her accomplishments her sensitivity to criticism was both singular and extreme and therefore highly dangerous to her well-being. For Clara to undertake any matters of importance, and she neither forgot nor forgave the failure of the United States to sign the Geneva Convention at once, she must somehow regain soundness of mind in a sound body. Otherwise the likelihood of fading into retirement was very real.

It is easy enough to mark the time and place of Clara Barton's new beginning. In 1876 she entered Dr. James Jackson's sanitarium in Dansville, Livingston County, New York. Jackson called his health clinic "Our Home On The Hillside." Established in the late 1850s, it had slowly gained a reputation, not for miracle cures, but for a regimen of nutritious foods, prescribed rest, and innocent recreation which, when followed over a period of time, produced marvelous restorative results. People commonly gained a new vitality and a new mental outlook. Early in the year Clara inquired of Dr. Jackson about the possibility of entering the sanitarium. Three months later, in March, she met a Miss Adams, a young woman from Worcester who had been a resident under Dr. Jackson's care. She told Clara it was "the place to get well."[2] Clara recorded in her diary that Miss Adams struck her "not as an enthusiast, but a calm, sensible girl; looks at things in the light of reason and common sense."[3] She pretty well convinced Barton what she must do to "get well" again. Despite the arduous trip to Dansville, Clara determined that it was worth a try. By early summer she had taken up residence at "Our Home On The Hillside" and was writing home cheerfully to cousin Elvira Stone about life there.

The sanitarium was nothing less than an oasis, ideally suited both to help Clara recover her health and as a place where she could be happy and content doing so. Indeed the ambiance and the cure were of one piece. After seven weeks she wrote that she could "find no occasion to regret coming. The place is simply beautiful in its location and surroundings." As for the other residents she admitted that she "never saw together any group of people that combines the degree of intellect, general intelligence, and culture as collected here." The staff of about fifty people she judged "skillful and competent." "Not one servant; the word nor the position is not known here." Clara rhapsodized about the food: fruit picked that day was on the table, an abundance of fresh vegetables, and new milk from the on-site dairy added to the pleasure of eating. A lecture hall for entertainments by the residents and visiting dignitaries, including Susan B. Anthony and Frederick Douglass, was another highlight of life on the hillside. Clara neatly and accurately summed up her impression when she wrote Elvira, "One has only to be lazy and be jolly and get well if you can."[4]

At first Barton lived in the main building, a structure that housed most of the three hundred patients. Later she moved into Dansville because she wanted a place of her own, adhering to the regimen laid down by Dr. Jackson nonetheless. After less than a year and a half Clara was again a well person. Her months under Jackson's care had given her ample time to assess the past in looking for meaning to the future. She once again commenced to correspond with various people of importance, including the Grand Duchess Louise. The reason for these letters, it appears, was twofold. As she regained her strength and equilibrium she wanted to share the good news with others whom she valued as friends. Her second purpose, though not ulterior, was to intimate her intention of returning to an active life of philanthropy. For example, she wrote to John D. DeFreize, recollecting a wartime friendship. DeFreize was now the public printer for the United States government. Clara asked him for his help in arranging a meeting with President Hayes, explaining that "Lately European people have laid upon my hands an international matter pertaining to humanity for which it seems proper that I see the President."[5] She was more explicit with Grand Duchess Louise. She told her about the prospect of using "my influence and the little strength I have" to promote United States participation in the work of the International Red Cross. She explained that she had written to Dr. Appia in Geneva to inquire if she could be of help in an "effort to establish an international organization in my own country for the collection and receipt of supplies, which could work under the insignia of the Red Cross." Her interest had been rekindled in part by rumors of an impending war between Russia and Turkey. But war or no war, Barton wanted her country under the banner of the Red Cross. If Dr. Appia sanctioned her request she went on to say that she would attempt to set up a headquarters "near or at New York." "Thus I would try to bring the early and organized efforts of America into direct communication with the activities of Europe." She was confident that this could be done. "Our people are generous, tender-hearted and quick in their sympathies."[6] Whatever the Establishment, and especially the State Department, might offer by way of objection Barton was convinced the populace would rally to favor and support her mission. The foundation and endeavors of an American

Red Cross Society became Clara's greatest cause, linked in law and spirit with the Geneva-based international organization.

For all of that these were only dreams put into words, a vow of action without certainty of fulfillment. The Civil War had ended more than a decade before; did the people still remember and cherish Clara Barton? Equally to the point, did she herself have the stamina which combined with a national stature would be essential to pull if off? It would be a mistake, in consequence, to assume that Barton had a well worked out strategy for achieving her goals. She knew full well what she wanted to do but was hesitant as to how she should proceed. In this respect Dr. Appia offered her sound advice in writing to her in June of 1877. He believed that Clara indeed "could become the soul" of the enterprise to bring the United States into the ranks of the Red Cross, but "medicine teaches us that a soul without a body has no life at all." Appia urged his "honored friend" to create the necessary body, an organization ready to "write, to arrange methodologies, to publish, to keep the correspondence, to collect, to buy, to receive visitors. . . . Surround yourself at once with a little body of persons of good will and capacity, docile to your directions, either women or young men, especially doctors." Following up on these exhortations Appia listed five steps that should be taken. Awaken the attention and sympathy of the public. Establish a correspondence with the International Committee. Contact directly the president of the United States. Raise funds through a public subscription. Finally, arrange to send two commissioners, perhaps two medical doctors recommended by the president, to go to Geneva.[7] In so far as Appia's proposals could be tailored to the prevailing situation in the United States Barton would be guided by these suggestions.

As a result of extensive correspondence between Barton and the Grand Duchess, Appia, and Gustave Moynier, events were set in motion that would culminate, years later, in United States association with the International Red Cross. Clara was appointed as the authorized agent for the International Committee, directed to make representations to appropriate American officials. She was delighted with the appointment, and received a letter from Moynier to be presented to President Hayes. Barton liked the idea of going straight to the top and was much pleased by Moynier's statement in the letter to be handed over to the president which read: "We have already an able and devoted assistant in Miss Clara Barton, to whom we confide the case of handing you this present request." In the letter Moynier was brief and to the point. After stressing the earnest desire of the committee that the United States become associated with the Geneva-based organization, he observed that it would be "irrational" not to have the approval of the American government before appealing to its citizens for support of Red Cross relief programs. Reminding the president that there had been an official United States representative at the 1864 conference in Geneva and referring to this as a "mark of approbation," Moynier added that the International Committee looked forward to a formal confirmation of America's respect for the principles of the convention. He expressed the hope that the president would take all necessary measures to bring this about and in conclusion wrote "we only wait such good news, Mr. President, in order to urge the founding of an American Society of the Red Cross."[8] Despite the previous refusal of the United States to sign the Convention Moynier could find no good reason why now it could not be accomplished.

Before arranging to visit the White House Barton prepared a brochure: *The Red Cross of the Geneva Convention: What It Is.* Written in language easy to understand because it was intended to have a circulation with the general public and with important members of the administration and the Congress, it proved to be a major document for introducing Red Cross principles to America. It stressed the humanitarian nature of its aims and objectives and underscored the fact that "the relief societies themselves are entirely national and independent, each one governing itself." The aim here was to try to defuse the previously voiced objection based on the "entangling alliance" phobia traditional to United States foreign policy. Barton noted the organization's major characteristics: centralization for efficiency of operations, preparation for readiness to meet emergencies, impartiality for aiding friend and foe alike, solidarity for the purpose of allowing nonbelligerent states to offer assistance. Finally, and of greatest significance for an American Red Cross, Barton announced that the Society would function as a peacetime agency, "offering ready succor and assistance to sufferers in time of national or widespread calamities, such as plague . . . devastating fires or floods, railroad disasters, mining catastrophes, etc."9 The dual purpose of war relief and peacetime aid was not original with Barton, Dunant having promoted the idea in Europe, but the peacetime factor had special appeal to Americans. The prospect of future wars in which the United States would be engaged seemed slim at that juncture but natural and manmade calamities were common. There was, in short, a compelling need for an American Red Cross Society here at home. Barton concluded her statement with an appeal that membership in the international organization was a matter of charity for the people and a matter of honor for the nation.

Clara was fully aware of how abruptly Secretary of State Seward had dismissed the proposal for American entry back in 1864. Now, however, conditions were different and her hopes were high. The nation was enjoying a period of relative calm after the wrenching experiences of the Civil War and the uncertainties that followed in the Reconstruction period. Perhaps more germane, the Red Cross had in Clara Barton a forceful, outspoken advocate for a cause that, because of her own exertions, was becoming better known and appreciated. As part of her tactics she importuned various members of the Hayes cabinet and she judged her reception by these ranking officials to range from interested to sympathetic. At the Interior Department Carl Schurz, a sometime refugee from the revolutions of 1848, was quite receptive to the European-born humanitarian purposes of the Red Cross. Richard Thompson, Secretary of the Navy, was equally attentive to Barton's words. The attorney general, Charles Devin, was particularly encouraging, telling Clara he perceived no legal obstacle; at the War Department Secretary McCreery "knew nothing of the Red Cross," Clara reported, "but thought its accession a well enough thing to do." None of the cabinet officials consulted raised any real objection which could only be taken as a good omen.10 Unfortunately Robert

Hale, Clara's cousin, a man with personal access to the State Department failed to try to persuade Secretary William Evarts to look favorably on Barton's petition. She was hurt and angered because she saw Evarts as a likely opponent.[11]

The meeting between President Hayes and Barton took place January 3, 1878. It was a cordial enough affair but from Clara's viewpoint not at all successful. Hayes had little knowledge of the Red Cross and displayed only a mild interest in hearing about it. When Barton handed him the letter from Moynier he read it, but was virtually without comment on its contents. After a few minutes the president excused himself, saying he had congressmen awaiting him in his office. Lucy Hayes, the president's wife who had been present throughout the meeting, exchanged a few words with Clara, presented her with a small bouquet of flowers and took her leave. There had been no meeting of minds. The only hopeful sign was Hayes's expressed intention of turning the request over to Secretary Evarts. His note to him, dated the next day, was far from an endorsement. It read: "Miss Barton of New York has some plans regarding the mitigation of the cruelties of war which she wishes to present to you. Please give her a hearing and such aid and encouragement as may be deemed by you fit."[12] It may be assumed the president did not want to be bothered, implying that his subordinate deal with the matter. Barton's prospects for agreement dimmed even more when she was unable to arrange to speak with Evarts. Instead the secretary referred the president's instruction to his subordinate, Frederick Seward, son of the former secretary of state and the man who had initially rejected the idea of United States participation in the work of the Red Cross. The position of the State Department was not going to budge: any such association was a violation of the spirit of the Monroe Doctrine just as it went against the advice of President Washington who long ago had warned against entangling alliances. Frederick Seward's words were entirely predictable and he put them with unsparing bluntness: "It is all settled, the question will never again be considered."[13] Barton came away from this encounter both wounded and resentful, but determined to see the issue through. She continued for several weeks more to politick and to preach to anyone in the capital who would give ear. Clara had never taken kindly to rejection, or no as a final answer. Her state of mind she summed up in a letter to Dr. Appia. "With that previous refusal in the way it will require great care, labor and perseverance to gain the point desired, but I shall not despair until I must."[14]

It seemed best, meanwhile, to return to her home in Dansville where she was to spend much of the remainder of 1878 and most of the next year as well. There she could regain some of her physical and mental strength, drained as she had been by the months of pleading and disappointment in Washington. At the same time she could plan strategy for the next round in the fight. In Dansville Barton's day-to-day routine was ordered and therapeutic. She gardened and planted trees, baked goodies, put up vegetables and fruits for the coming winter, and had a kitten soon-to-be-cat, named Tommy, a happy distraction. She concluded that propaganda taken in its generic meaning, that is, dissemination of information designed to persuade people to act, could be done as well from Dansville as elsewhere. The Hayes administration had now been written off, and Clara was hardly disappointed to learn that the Republican Party had refused to nominate him for a second term. Any change in the administration promised fresh faces and perhaps sympathetic hearts and minds on the subject of the United States as a signatory to the Geneva Convention. Even so, Clara entertained no false hopes. The ground had to be prepared more carefully than before, her message had to be gotten to the people as well as to the powerful in and out of government. As she told Appia "great care, labor and perseverance" were her marching orders. Clara liked using military terminology to express her position, and there was one interest group to whom she could turn with good effect, the Grand Army of the Republic (GAR).

By giving her attention to the GAR she was beginning anew to marshal her forces. The Grand Army of the Republic was the Union veterans organization that had already shown itself to be a powerful voting bloc when an issue was stated in such a way as to arouse the erstwhile "boys in blue." "Waving the bloody shirt of rebellion" in consequence had been a favorite ploy of politicians. It was a tactic

Barton understood and was prepared to use. She wanted "her boys" to remember their suffering, to remind them of what wars meant to the private soldier, and thereby to stir their support for a society that stood to ameliorate the distress of men in future wars. It was only natural that Clara would seek out John Logan, a Civil War general and the man who first organized the GAR, serving as its president for several years. At the annual encampments of the veterans there was political hay to be made. She felt she badly needed veterans' support; she was not disappointed. Logan was there when she needed him as were other generals, Ben Butler, Phil Sheridan, and James A. Garfield among them. Garfield would be of the utmost value. Barton strongly backed his presidential candidacy, waxing enthusiastic to one correspondent in describing him as "a statesman, a man of firmness, culture, courage, physical and moral—just, humane and of unimpeachable integrity of character."[15] In private and in public Clara raised her voice, hailing Garfield as the next president, convinced that he would look kindly on the United States as a member of the international Red Cross. If the number of voters in the overall count who actually heard her was small, newspapers in New York and New England carried the message to many more. As she was to recall, in 1880 she undertook to do a lot of "what might be called Public Writing."[16]

Barton's friendship with two newspaper men, Walter Phillips and George Kennan, dovetailed with plans to build up popular interest. Phillips was in charge of the Washington office of the Associated Press and thus in a unique position to give favorable coverage to the various persons and activities that were part of Barton's campaign of information. As it happened both men were themselves enthusiastic about the purpose and principles of the Red Cross. Local newspapers also took up the cry, the Dansville *Advertizer*, as might be expected, the Providence *Daily Journal*, and the Worcester *Spy*. The election of Garfield in 1880, though not a guarantee of anything, was nonetheless a promise of everything if "great care, labor and perseverance" remained her watchwords.

President Garfield received Clara Barton at the end of March. She came close to inviting herself by reason of a respectful but strongly worded letter sent to the White House in February. Garfield's reply was encouraging. Once again Gustave Moynier's letter of 1877, expressing the anticipated pleasure of welcoming the United States into the ranks of the Red Cross, was handed over to an American president. This time the response was one of "warm, personal interest."[17] After some Civil War reminiscing, the president assured Barton that the matter would be given over to Secretary of State James G. Blaine. Within days an interview with Blaine was arranged. It was a memorable occasion. Indeed, this may have been Blaine, the political animal, at his most sincere, as William Barton's detailed account bears out.

Blaine began the meeting with an apology: he had kept Clara and her nephew Stephen waiting over an hour. At first Blaine wondered if the concerns of his department were peripheral to the issue, believing the War Department might better be consulted. Only when Clara stressed the international implications and the need for a treaty by recounting the reasons why Seward and his successors had rebuffed her, did he take her point. Blaine assured her that he wanted to hear the full story of the Red Cross, saying "I can give you all the time you need." Barton then told the story of the Red Cross in great detail, revealing at the same time her unwavering commitment to it.

When he next spoke, Blaine dismissed the obstacle of the Monroe Doctrine as pertinent to the issue as readily as Seward, Hamilton Fish (Grant's secretary of state), and Evarts had invoked it. "The Monroe Doctrine was not made to ward off humanity . . . the grounds for Mr. Seward's objection would not stand in the way of the present administration." The secretary added that he was "in full sympathy" with Moynier's proposal and "would cooperate fully with her in carrying the matter successfully through." And that was not all. He informed Clara that he would so indicate to Moynier by letter. When Barton entered a cautionary word about the requirement of senatorial approval of the treaty, the expansive Blaine grew more confident, saying, "if it needed the action of the Senate, that could be had."[18] With the close of their discussion Clara was euphoric, a state of emotion that continued into the following day when she spoke with secretary of war, Robert Todd Lincoln. Lincoln felt able to assure her the War Department would do its part to help bring about American adhesion to the Geneva Convention.[19]

Immediately Barton turned to the Senate, lobbying her proposal there to good effect because she could vouch for the backing of Garfield and Blaine. Senator Omar D. Conger of Michigan, whose brother Barton had attended to during the war, was among its strongest boosters. It was Conger who, on May 17, 1881, introduced on the floor of the Senate the following resolution.

Resolved that the Secretary of State be requested to furnish to the Senate copies (translations) of the Articles of Convention signed at Geneva, Switzerland, August 22, 1864, touching the treatment of those wounded in war, together with the forms of ratification employed by the several Governments, parties thereto.[20]

As these papers were being gathered, Blaine wrote a reassuring letter to Barton. With Moynier's communication to the president in mind, he asked Clara to inform Geneva of the sentiments of President Garfield and his officers of government, saying that they were in "full sympathy with any wise measures tending toward the amelioration of the suffering incident to warfare." After explaining that the Constitution of the United States required that certain powers, especially the power to make war, were carefully reserved to the Congress, he hastened to add, "I will be happy to give any measures which you may propose careful attention and consideration . . . and should the President as I doubt not he will, approve of the matter, the Administration will recommend to Congress the adoption of the international treaty you desire."[21] Clara Barton had become a conduit for the flow of information and policy intention between Washington and Geneva.

Within the month Moynier replied to the secretary of state. He expressed "much satisfaction" with the news he had received. He thanked Blaine and President Garfield "for having been willing to take into serious consideration the wish contained in my letter of August

19, 1877, assured a very natural wish, since it tended to unite your country with a work of charity and civilization for which it is one of the best qualified." After pointing out that several countries had lately signed the Convention, all South American nations: Peru, Chile, Bolivia, and Argentina, Moynier concluded with a renewed expression of hope that the United States would join these sister American states.[22]

Hope was slow to ripen into reality. It would be almost a year before the United States finally agreed to the terms of the Geneva Convention, a period of tension following the shooting of President Garfield in July, his lingering death struggle and his demise in September. The president had been the key figure at this stage of Barton's campaign, but the views of his successor, Chester Alan Arthur, when it came to the Red Cross, were unknown. To complicate the prospects Secretary Blaine announced that he would be leaving the State Department at the end of December, his replacement still to be named. More delay could be expected and the outcome still clouded in uncertainty. Weary to the edge of exhaustion Clara concluded that only steady pressure applied to the public and politicos alike would salvage her dream.

Some measures, looking to sustain the tide that had been running in her favor, Barton had already taken. In May she had called a meeting of chief supporters, her purpose to move to incorporate the Society of the Red Cross under the laws of the District of Columbia. This would give the fledgling organization a much needed legal standing. Barton's name was on the letterhead she sent out to those she was counting on for help; she was described as the "American Representative" of the International Red Cross. A president for the American society would be required but both President Garfield and his wife declined to serve. At first this was a disappointment to Clara because heads of state in Europe had assumed leadership or at least patronage of the Red Cross societies there. The president, instead nominated Clara Barton for the presidency, a gracious gesture to which she agreed. Judge William Lawrence who had worked closely with Barton in writing a constitution for the American Society was elected vice-president. All in all this was an important preliminary step toward integration with the international body.

The approaching finalization tended to draw fire from an unexpected quarter. The Women's National Relief Association, also known as the Blue Anchor from the symbol used to identify the movement, was dedicated to the same sort of relief activities as the Red Cross; a great many of its associates were women of the upper class. If Clara never laid claim to being the exclusive American agent of humanitarian aid—after all, she had worked with the Sanitary Commission during the war and admired the labors of Frances Gage, Dorothea Dix, and other women—she did insist that her society and hers alone should be recognized by the committee in Geneva. It appears that the Blue Anchor had exactly that in mind for itself. With the efforts of the Blue Anchor moving in that direction after the death of Garfield and before any action by the Senate, Clara had reason to worry. She countered by seeking to win backers. At the annual encampment of the GAR in 1881, General Logan urged endorsement of Clara Barton's society, ignoring any rival. Equally if not more valuable to her cause was her cordial relationship with Moynier and Appia who had no intention of turning to anyone else. They were Clara's admirers and confidants; to them it would be unthinkable to betray her. Determined to build her case Barton went ahead and established the first local chapter of the now incorporated American Society of the Red Cross in Dansville and soon thereafter chapters came into being in Rochester and Syracuse. The embryonic Red Cross had an opportunity to show its stuff when a forest fire did great damage in Michigan in the autumn. Barton was quickly at the task of organizing aid, gathering a full range of items, with boxes of tools, clothing, and medicine sent off to the troubled area. She appointed Julian Hubbell as field agent, a young medical student and a recently enlisted faithful follower. It was during these same months that Clara with the help and guidance of Joseph Sheldon wrote an expanded pamphlet dealing with the work of the Red Cross. She made sure that the five thousand copies were widely distributed, paying for them out of pocket. Combined with ongoing favorable newspaper coverage this helped to keep both Clara and her cause before the public and the Washington Establishment.

The spell of doubt was partly broken in December. President Arthur in his annual address to the Congress was pointed in his remarks. Reminding the Congress that the Senate previously had asked for the text of the Geneva Convention, he now urged its acceptance. "I trust," he said, "that this action foreshadows such interest in the subject as will result in the adhesion of the United States to that humane and commendable engagement."[23] The phrasing was labored but the intention was clear. After December things went smoothly forward. The Senate Committee on Foreign Relations having heard the testimony of Miss Barton voted unanimously to send the treaty on to the full house for consideration. Outgoing Secretary Blaine reiterated his recommendation. Doubt about the outcome all but disappeared. On February 6, during one of her periodic visits to the State Department she met with the new secretary, Frederick T. Frelinghuysen. He directed an assistant to show Clara an unbound sheaf of papers. Admitting that it was somewhat irregular, this Mr. Brown handed over for examination the text of the treaty that would be considered by the Senate. When she finished reading every word of the document she was asked if it met with her approval. "It is all I could ask for," she replied.[24] It would soon be the law of the land. President Arthur signed the treaty on March 1. On the sixteenth Senator Lapham wrote to Barton of having the "gratifying privilege of informing you of the ratification by the Senate of the Geneva Convention; of the full assent of the United States to the same."[25] From Geneva Moynier, upon hearing the news, was full of congratulations, making this point: "It is your society alone and none other that we will patronize."[26] The treaty ratified, only then did Clara realize how "weak" and "broken" the ordeal had made her.[27]

The treaty was to have but limited significance in overall American foreign policy development. It was not a harbinger of new directions for that policy. The Monroe Doctrine had not been seriously breached or even reinterpreted. That doctrine, largely symbolic and rarely invoked, would be reaffirmed and expanded during the 1890s with

American involvement in the Venezuelan boundary dispute in 1895
and in the days of Theodore Roosevelt as president, by the Roosevelt
Corollary to the Monroe Doctrine in 1904. Still, ratification of the
treaty marked a *volte face*, given the obduracy of Seward, Fish, and
Evarts. What accounted for the change? Was it a question of Garfield's
statesmanship or Blaine's indifference to established policy? Why was
President Arthur so amenable? Was he attempting to lessen the tarnish
on American honor brought about by the senseless murder of Garfield, or was he merely following Garfield's lead? Did the adherence
of Argentina, Bolivia, Chile, and Peru have any influence, these sister
American states? Or was it a more general consideration, an expression
of what appeared to be, falsely as it turned out, an example of more
civilized rules for future conflicts among the powers? As pertinent as
such questions may or may not be, they tend to obscure the genius of
Clara Barton who, extravagant as it may sound, had bent political and
public opinion to her idealism and to her will.

## NOTES

1. William E. Barton, *The Life of Clara Barton*, 2 vols., New York:
AMS Press, 1969, vol. 2, p. 90.
2. Barton Journal, March 16, 1876, Clara Barton *Papers*, Library of
Congress.
3. William E. Barton, *The Life of Clara Barton*, vol. 2, p. 93.
4. Barton to Elvira Stone, July 15, 1876, Clara Barton *Papers*.
5. Barton to John D. DeFreize, Sept. 8, 1877, Clara Barton *Papers*.
6. Barton to Grand Duchess Louise, May 18, 1877, Clara Barton
*Papers*.
7. Louis Appia to Barton, June 14, 1877, William E. Barton, *The Life
of Clara Barton*, vol. 2, pp. 126–130.
8. Moynier to Barton, Aug. 19, 1877, Ishbel Ross, *Clara Barton: Angel
of the Battlefield,* Indianapolis: Bobbs Merrill, 1949, Appendix 2, pp. 273–
78.
9. Ibid., Appendix 2, pp. 274–78.
10. Blanche C. Williams, *Clara Barton: Daughter of Destiny*, Philadelphia: J. P. Lippincott Company, 1941, p. 202.
11. Ibid., p. 241.

12. Ross, *Angel of the Battlefield*, p. 133.

13. Ibid.

14. Williams, *Daughter of Destiny*, p. 240.

15. Barton to Gustave Bergmann, Dec. 26, 1880, Ross, *Angel of the Battlefield*, p. 135.

16. Williams, *Daughter of Destiny*, p. 250.

17. William E. Barton, *The Life of Clara Barton*, vol. 2, p. 149.

18. Ibid.

19. Pryor, *Professional Angel*, p. 203.

20. William E. Barton, *The Life of Clara Barton*, vol. 2, p. 152.

21. James G. Blaine to Barton, May 20, 1881, ibid., p. 153.

22. Gustave Moynier to James G. Blaine, ibid., p. 154.

23. President Arthur's "Message to Congress," December, 1881, Pryor, *Professional Angel*, p. 209.

24. Ross, *Angel of the Battlefield*, p. 145.

25. E. S. Lapham to Barton, March 16, 1882, Clara Barton *Papers*.

26. Ross, *Angel of the Battlefield*, p. 145.

27. Barton Journal, March 10 and 16, 1882, Clara Barton *Papers*.

# — 5 —

# *The Red Cross: What It Became*

Clara Barton was the founder of the American Red Cross. She was also the architect—the design would be what she wanted it to be—and its builder—she would provide the leadership and not merely the inspiration required to carry out the tasks that by nature and by nations were set before her. In 1882 the Red Cross was largely a paper organization with a promise of achievement. For the next twenty years Barton labored to fulfill the promise, and in the event she exceeded expectations rather much as she had done all her life.

The problems facing the newly born society were serious in nature. It had no working organization. At this stage Clara Barton was the Red Cross and the Red Cross was Clara Barton. Headquarters in Washington were located in the residence Barton had purchased in 1878, a row house at 947 T Street in the northwest quadrant of the city. There were only three local chapters, all in New York state, at Dansville, Rochester, and Syracuse, though others would soon come into being. Further, the society had no operating funds and slim prospects that financial support would be forthcoming. The idea that the Congress would appropriate even a modest annual stipend was far-fetched. For a society with national pretensions based on international recognition, extended on June 9, 1882, there were good reasons to doubt, not its survival perhaps, but certainly its great success. The Blue Anchor, for example, was busy as ever collecting money from private sources and distributing its largesse to distressed areas in Michigan and Mississippi. Better financed than Barton's group, it had to be taken as a serious rival. Still another problem casting doubt on the future prosperity of the Red Cross was, ironically, Clara herself. She has been described both as the strength and the weakness of the American society during its early history. Barton was indefatigable in promoting the Red Cross, "her child" as she often spoke of it, and this was its greatest asset. Her domination of the organization also proved a weakness, as it led to methods of administration that alienated important people whose support would have bolstered its reputation and enabled it better to carry out its mission.[1] The Red Cross from 1882 down to 1904, the year she relinquished leadership, bore Clara Barton's inimitable stamp. Absolutely vital to its early successes she was seen as standing in the path of continued growth. Nothing, however, should be allowed to obscure the accomplishments that must be credited to Barton during her years of ascendancy. The American Red Cross was bone of her bone, and spirit of her spirit.[2]

Lives rarely move on straight, smooth lines, and Clara Barton's was no exception. That she would pursue the work of the Red Cross was hardly to be doubted, the evidence of it is altogether convincing. There would be roadblocks and detours nonetheless. A forest fire in Michigan in 1881, a time when the society was embryonic, was the first test. "Nothing could give our association more standing and popularity than to issue a call upon local societies to aid in the present emergency," she was to tell Judge Lawrence.[3] The whole episode foreshadowed the methods of the Red Cross in years to come, revealing its appeal and its strength in the grassroots nature of its operation. National headquarters sent appeals to the local societies, whether the aid was needed in their locales or elsewhere, and the chapters responded. In this first instance, the Michigan forest fire, donations from Dansville and Rochester, places remote from the trouble spot, were generous offerings of money and supplies. Barton envisioned her role as that of coordinator, recognizing the centrifugal realities. Just as government in the United States in the 1880s and 1890s remained largely contained in the states, so the power of the Red Cross resided in the local societies.

To put this principle into action, Barton sent her field agents, Mark Bunnell, a Dansville native, and Julian Hubbell, the Barton convert, to the Michigan disaster areas. Bunnell proved a passing figure; in contrast Hubbell grew to be a key player, completely dedicated to Clara and the Red Cross, no doubt viewing them as one and the same. The success of this initial Red Cross undertaking, if limited, was nonetheless a matter of pride and importance to an organization requiring a good public image if it were to carry out its mission successfully. Though Michiganders through many group endeavors came to the aid of their fellow citizens, the insignia of the Red Cross did not go unnoticed.

A fresh disaster, flooding along the Mississippi in the spring of 1882 meant a fresh opportunity to help and to be noticed. Again Barton dispatched Julian Hubbell, at the time still a medical student at the University of Michigan, to the south to survey the damages and the essential needs of the populace in the troubled areas. Appeals to chapters up north received an encouraging response but the amount of money and goods actually collected was modest. The assistance given by the United States army simply dwarfed the activity of the Red Cross by its distribution of army rations and the provision of tents to shelter the homeless. Still there was opportunity for favorable publicity for the Red Cross, and Hubbell did an excellent job of promoting its image. Due largely to his urging, chapters were established along the Mississippi at New Orleans, Vicksburg, and Natchez. By being in the field Hubbell not only raised the profile of the Red Cross, but he showed himself indispensable to Barton who found him both devoted and trustworthy. The two made a remarkable team in the years to come, with Hubbell's medical degree an added advantage.

Natural calamities played into the hands of Clara Barton in these very early years of growth. When a few weeks after the Mississippi flooding the Ohio Valley was under water with damaging effects Hubbell was again on the scene. With his help chapters were founded in Cincinnati, Louisville, and St. Louis. It was as though fire or flood was a preliminary to the spread of local organizations. In Barton's own words "we are constantly growing, both in usefulness and appreciation."[4] The straight line along which Clara's leadership appeared to be proceeding was, however, to make a sharp and unexpected detour. Years later she was to recall it as the most foolish step she was ever induced to take.[5]

It was in January of 1883 that Barton received a letter from her old wartime friend and patron, General Benjamin Butler. Butler was now governor of Massachusetts and found himself the target of attacks by advocates of prison reform. Ben Butler was no reformer and was never likely to be one. He was the very opposite, a heavy-handed critic of the prison system that he thought was expensive and inefficient. This placed him in opposition to much informed opinion that held the Massachusetts penal methods were worthy of emulation by other states. Butler was politically vulnerable as a result. He believed he saw a way out of this self-imposed danger by calling on Clara Barton, a name well known in Massachusetts, to head up the Reformatory Prison for Women at Sherborn which he had previously threatened to shut down. Barton's disposition was always inclined to try to help those who at one time had helped her, and Butler had been a true friend and supporter of her Civil War work, perhaps her staunchest advocate among the general officers. Was Butler asking too much of the Angel of the Battlefield who at the time was fully engaged in fighting the battles of the Red Cross? At first Clara thought so. Reasons not to accept the general's invitation were obvious. Such an undertaking would surely separate her from the active leadership of the Red Cross at a critical time in its development. Secondly, she had no knowledge of, much less experience in prison management, or of prison psychology. Thirdly, a woman succeeding a woman (Dr. Eliza Mosher) in the position might bring down political fire on her by the antifeminists; or she might be made to appear as a mere sop by the reformers.

Barton's initial response to Butler was that she needed time to consider the offer. To gain a better awareness of what the position required, she made a trip to inspect the Sherborn facility in late

January. There was an opportunity to do some good, of that there was no doubt, a consideration that counted much with her. Despite this and her abiding respect for General Butler, Clara declined the superintendency. The next month he was in Washington, met Barton, and accompanied her to the White House in hopes of persuading President Arthur to support a federal grant of funds to the Red Cross. In this way the general broke through Clara's defenses. Before finally agreeing to accept the headship of the prison she laid down two conditions: that she would occupy the office for six months and only six months, and that she would be spared any and all involvement in the politics of the rival parties in the state. Barton's appointment was confirmed and she arrived to take up her duties on May 1.

At the end of her time on the job Barton submitted a report of her superintendency, one that throws light on the nature of the prison as well as to her response to the plight of the women incarcerated there. In this latter regard, she was both sympathetic to the fate of the inmates and willing to defend them as a class of unfortunate human beings. Barton took particular exception to the treatment of the women as criminals when "not a one-fourth part . . . are guilty of or convicted of any real crime. . . . Yet the poor, helpless, mis-guided, rum-drenched women are sentenced to the same servitude, and are subjected to the same code of discipline and go out with the same brand of shame upon their brow [as the] men of Concord [prison] where every inmate is convicted of a crime."[6] Barton continued what was a feminist attack on the penal system. To her the women at Sherborn were "more weak than wicked, more often sinned against than sinning." In consequence she called for a "parental, maternal system of government, and to this they [the inmates] were all amenable; even the most obstinate yields to the rule of kindness, firmly and steadily administered."[7] In a word, Barton brought to her administration a belief in the basic goodness of those she was responsible for supervising, and had acted accordingly. In writing all this, Clara was not so much consciously feminist as she was humanitarian, yet her words appealed to those who divined a double standard of justice for men and women and who were fighting against it.

Drawing on experiences at Sherborn, Barton sounded still another note that had a strongly feminist ring to it, an attack on the liquor trade. The grog shop and the brothel were to her the twin sources of female degradation. As she told one group of legislators who were inspecting Sherborn: "any time when you will find a way to make it impossible for the people of the State to get intoxicating liquor upon which to get drunk, I will guarantee you that in six months the State of Massachusetts may rent Sherborn for a shoe factory."[8] And she went on. "In *this* country I regard drunkenness as the grandfather of crime, and the mother of prisons, almshouses, asylums and workhouses, the parents of vice and want, and the instigator of murder."[9] Clearly Barton was contending that it was the environment from which the individual sprang as much as any bad seed that made for crime. It followed then that by maintaining the environment of the reformatory as positive and encouraging, those who had served their time would be more likely to try to lead proper lives in the future.

The official responsibilities of the administrator at Sherborn were to care for some two hundred fifty inmates and to supervise a staff of thirty that included a medical doctor and a chaplain. All this required a considerable amount of paperwork. There was correspondence to attend to: letters from relatives of inmates to be answered, communications to the State Commission on Prisons, and information supplied to advocates of prison reform. Record keeping was another administrative staple: records pertaining to food ordered and delivered, of maintenance and improvements under contract to the state, and of course records of inmate behavior. As time-consuming and preoccupying as such matters were, Barton took a motherly interest in her charges. The women were aware of her great reputation for wartime service, and she gladly shared her memories of the war in weekly talks given in the chapel. The inmates held her in awe and in turn they were treated with dignity and respect. To promote communication Barton provided a suggestion box where one was free to complain or make a request. As women left the prison having served their sentences, they often wept and took Clara's hand, promising to lead the better way of life that she had pointed them to. Both administratively and as a place where reform of the inmates was truly an objective, Barton's tenure at Sherborn deserves to be pronounced a success.

Perhaps one reason for this was that Clara was virtually in complete charge of the situation, an arrangement suitable to her temperament then as always. There was no one to challenge her, save perhaps the chaplain who entertained a much lower regard for the character of the women, but whom Clara simply ignored. More fundamental still was her genuine compassion for the unfortunate women she encountered. They were the real victims of society, and society remained blind to that fact. The women had touched her heart much as "her boys" had done in the war. Both found themselves subjected to forces beyond their control, both crying out for help and understanding. In some ways then the days at Sherborn were immensely satisfying but on the whole Barton was as anxious to end her six months in office as she had been reluctant to take up her duties originally. As it happened she stayed an additional two months on the job, exiting at the end of 1883 when General Butler gave up the governorship. His final words to Barton: "In what you have done in the prison . . . it has become an institution of which the State may well be proud"[10] echoed the sentiments of reformers and nonreformers alike.

The new year, 1884, turned out to be a demanding one for Barton and the American Red Cross. Clara was quickly back at her post as president, cognizant that during her days at Sherborn the ship had drifted, with little to show by way of advance or progress. So low had the society slipped in the public consciousness that some physicians in Philadelphia believed the organization to be defunct, and had approached the international body at Geneva proposing to revive it. With Barton back in command that would change. In February floods along the Ohio and Mississippi provided the Red Cross, *deus ex machina*, with opportunities to demonstrate an ability to respond to crises almost immediately. Eighteen eighty-four was also the year Clara traveled to Geneva to attend the Third International Red Cross Conference, marking the twentieth anniversary of the creation of the Geneva Convention. Clara was something of a cynosure at the gathering, the only female representative of a signatory nation and that in itself made her remarked upon. She was also a celebrity in her own right, something she greatly enjoyed. Few at home or abroad doubted henceforth the purpose and spirit of American participation in the mission of the international body, despite the years' long delay in American ratification.

The towering figure of Clara Barton cannot be allowed to overshadow completely contributions made by others as the American society carried on its relief efforts. Of these none is more worthy of note than Julian Hubbell. An Iowa native he had heard tales of Barton's Civil War exploits and came to worship her from afar. When the two met in Dansville, where he had taken a teaching position, Hubbell was immediately under Clara's spell. Because of her advice he left teaching to take up the study of medicine. Along the way, of course, he had served as Barton's field agent and troubleshooter at the time of the Michigan forest fire and the Mississippi Valley floods. A combination of medical skill, field experience, and total devotion to both Barton and the ideals of the Red Cross enabled Hubbell to make a singular contribution to their common cause. The following account of Hubbell's decision to commit himself to Barton is entirely believable. In January, 1884, Barton put the question to him: "Well, Julian, do you still want to work for me?" "More than anything else," he replied. "You will find the work harder than in the Michigan fires or Mississippi overflows." "I am young, strong and just thirty-six," he went on to explain. "I shall need your youth," Clara said. "Bring your trunk and take a room in my Washington home."[11] Thus was the bargain sealed. As with Barton herself Julian Hubbell came into his own by reason of his untiring exertions in combatting the floods of 1884. If after a while Barton tended to take him for granted, Dr. Hubbell, the true humanitarian, was content, neither craving nor needing public acclaim.[12]

Spring floods were all but an annual phenomenon for the great inland river system of North America that drained giant rivers and their tributaries into the Gulf of Mexico. Whether due to heavy, persistent rains or rapidly melting winter snows the Ohio, Missouri, and Mississippi Rivers often went out of control. Some years the damage and dislocations were slight. At other times the blows struck by nature were heavy and the results for man and beast, house and farm, were devastating. Such was the situation along the Ohio in February, 1884. Calls for help went out immediately and the Red Cross was attuned to the alert. This time Barton was not content to send agents into the disaster locales. She and Hubbell set out for Pittsburgh at once and then proceeded down the Ohio to assess the damage and what could be done to help those in distress.

The destruction was widespread, relief by the Red Cross would be in demand and much, it was thought, could be done to ease the suffering of the people and their communities. How to go about it was the first question to answer. Barton determined that the river itself could be turned from being an enemy to an ally. But for that to happen supply bases would have to be established. Barton and Hubbell agreed that the two most likely places were Cincinnati and Evansville in Indiana. Operational methods remained basic, reminiscent of those used by Barton during the Civil War. Appeals were sent out for donations of food and fodder and fuel along with farm implements and cash, all of this to be concentrated in warehouses rented in the two chief river towns. From these central points handouts could be made up and down the river using the Ohio as the main artery of transportation. "We must take to the water," Clara dryly observed.[13] To accomplish this a sizeable riverboat was required. At Evansville the *Josh V. Throop* (named for its owner) was chartered. A cross, hammered from iron and painted red, was strung between two smokestacks, proclaiming the presence of the Red Cross. Clara and her team, that included Hubbell, Enola Lee who was from Evansville, and Mahala Chaddock from Dansville, went into action.

The Congress had voted half a million dollars in relief money, and the army was heavily committed to the job of alleviating fear and uncertainty while rescuing stranded farmers and feeding hungry people. The army was not a competitor for Clara but a compatriot. Nonetheless she believed that she had a better feel for what was needed than some inexperienced army officers. The *Josh V. Throop* was a vessel small enough to be able to put in close to shore to aid those who might be isolated on their farms. In this way many families remote from the towns and villages received food and coal, warm blankets, and if deemed necessary, small amounts of cash. As before the Red Cross was wary about passing out money when what the people really needed was *things*. Things could be as insignificant as needle and thread, as well as hoes and shovels. Clara put great value on things.[14] The appreciation shown by those so aided was extremely satisfying to Barton and her associates. Added gratification came from the press reports flowing back to the eastern cities along with published thanks expressed in the area newspapers. The Red Cross was getting the kind of notice Barton had long held it should have because only through publicity could the society obtain the level of support it required to emerge as the country's chief, private relief agency. And that was Clara's aim all along. That its reputation was growing was evident from the amount of assistance it received in dollar value in 1884 when compared to what it had been able to realize just two years before. In 1882 when Hubbell had directed flood relief along the Mississippi approximately eight thousand dollars in goods and cash had been raised; in 1884 in what was admittedly a more serious crisis, the total figure stood at $175,000.

By late March the heavy rush of water along the Ohio had subsided as the Mississippi Valley prepared to battle the flooding from the north. Levees were crumbling and acres of cotton and sugar crops were inundated. Barton made a predictable decision: to go where the disaster was most acute. Reaching St. Louis she again chartered a boat, the *Mattie Belle*, and loaded it with every conceivable useful *thing*. Her reputation preceded her and was in fact greatly enhanced every time the *Mattie Belle* pulled close to land where seeds, tools, nails, clothing, and food were dropped off. Barton wanted to see current distress alleviated, but she also sought to encourage the people to think of rebuilding, and then to go ahead and do it. She was especially concerned that some part of the bounty be shared by hundreds of black families living close to the Mississippi. As communities set up committees to supervise the handing out of supplies, Barton was known to insist that there be field agents assigned to look after the interests of the former bondspeople.[15]

Barton could not but be aware that as she went farther and farther south she was deeper and deeper into what was once rebel territory. Despite her memories of Fredericksburg and Andersonville, she felt that the wounds of war were all but healed and that aid pouring in from all parts of the country must snuff out the last embers of hostility. Her mercy ship put in at many small wharfs and it was always welcome, though there was no mistaking Clara's Yankee accent. Arriving at Natchez on Easter morning she was shown the gentlest of southern hospitality. Days later at New Orleans she was feted as "an angel" sent by God. Soon it was back to Evansville and the Ohio. The *Josh V. Throop*, still displaying its red cross, was pressed into service. Loaded with items ranging from seeds to pots and pans to farm tools to lumber the task of lessening pain and encouraging hope went on.

Publicity continued to be highly favorable. Newspapers and Clara herself made much of a donation of $51.25 by six school children from Waterford in northwestern Pennsylvania, money raised by the young ones themselves. "The Little Six" became a symbol of Americans of all ages working for the common good through the offices of the Red Cross.

Barton and her helpers had spent over four months on the rivers and as exhilarating as it all was, Clara was exhausted. Happy that the Red Cross had acquitted itself as an effective relief agency she looked forward to the future. She spelled out her mood to Adolphus Solomons, a Washington businessman and one of her earliest boosters. "We have tested its power and ability to sustain and encourage. . . . We have proved that the Red Cross can start instantly, in small funds, without procrastination . . . sustaining itself through the heaviest campaign . . . and come out firm financially and socially with unblemished confidence and undisturbed integrity."[16] In her enthusiasm Clara had neither deceived herself nor exaggerated her triumph. It now remained for her friends in Geneva to salute her.

The Third International Conference of the Red Cross was scheduled to convene in Geneva in September. Clara had but a few weeks to recoup her strength and decided that she would be better rested were she to leave Washington for Dansville. At first she had no thought of attending the Geneva sessions. But while still in Washington, Secretary of State Frelinghuysen approached her, and urged her to be the senior United States representative. When she protested that her health was unlikely to permit her to attend, the secretary replied that he thought the sea air could only promote her recovery. Despite these playful words, Frelinghuysen held it imperative that the nation be represented by no one less than Clara Barton. Before departing for Dansville she agreed and as the secretary predicted she did not regret it. On the journey and while in Europe she relied very much on Judge Sheldon and Solomons who at the time was the treasurer of the American Society.

Though the years had passed since 1870–1871 Gustave Moynier and Louis Appia were still the major officials on the International Committee, and they greeted Barton in such a warm and reassuring fashion that she was made comfortable at once. There was never any pressure on her. Mere mention of the Barton name brought applause and whenever she appeared at a meeting or a social gathering there was a stir. At the close of the conference the Italian delegate rushed to the platform and proposed a vote of thanks to Barton because she "deserved well of humanity."[17] Sheldon wrote Julian Hubbell that Clara at Geneva was "a triumphant success."[18]

More substantive developments during the conference added to Barton's stature within the Red Cross community, namely, the formal adoption of the American Amendment to the original Geneva Treaty. It might well be termed the Barton Amendment. Judge Sheldon addressed the conference in urging acceptance of the policy that relief services should be available in peacetime as well as during wars. Several national societies were strongly in favor of this, but others hesitated, seeing it as a departure from the purposes set down for the Red Cross in 1864. Sheldon's arguments were strongly yet prudently stated. He was able to describe in gripping detail how in that very year the American Red Cross had brought aid and encouragement to thousands made hungry and homeless by the Ohio and Mississippi floods.

He was at pains to tell of Barton's leadership, how she was a living embodiment of the American Amendment. The judge went on to say that the Red Cross might founder in America if the amendment failed to win approval. As it had proved its worth, so it should be incorporated into the Convention, with each country free to exercise the option should it choose.[19] Originally the idea of Dunant, Barton had nurtured it to full flower. With Clara so intimately involved and given her standing with the other delegates, the American Amendment was easily adopted when the voting took place. Again the focus had been on this lone woman, the only female delegate, one enjoying equal rank with all the others. If Clara did not ordinarily think in feminist terms, many looked admiringly to her quiet leadership, believing it anticipated the day when other women of talent and ability would be in positions of authority. Barton's womanhood was widely and favorably commented on not because she was a duchess or a royal consort but because of what she had accomplished as an individual. As far as Clara was concerned if her presence in Geneva helped the cause of female emancipation, so much the better. She had long been in favor of free womanhood without consciously working toward it. Her attitude in this matter would cause misunderstanding and even criticism but her position continued unchanged. She wanted to be of service to all, men and women alike, when they needed aid and comfort. This was her creed, and this was her practice.

Upon the adjournment of the conference Barton remained some weeks on the Continent. She was a delegate to the Universal Peace Union holding its meetings in Geneva hard on the heels of the Red Cross convention. Of course she must visit Grand Duchess Louise in Karlsruhe, and there she met Empress Augusta, consort of Kaiser Wilhelm I of Germany. She continued to be a center of attention at the Badisch court. It was the kind of social climate Clara always enjoyed: esteem without criticism, and on her part an eagerness to please. By year's end she had traveled home via London, renewing friendships there. Looking back on 1884 it was a watershed year. Its accumulated reputation and good will Clara and the Red Cross would have reason to draw on heavily in the years just ahead.

Clara Barton had achieved full celebrity status by the mid-1880s. It was no longer a matter of fame such as she had known for two decades. Now she was renowned and revered at home and abroad. This change in status was a subtle one but it carried with it outward manifestations. It was now important to be seen, to be part of great public gatherings. At the Cotton Centennial Exposition held at New Orleans in December, 1884, Clara attended the opening festivities; she and Julian Hubbell prepared a Red Cross exhibit. It centered on a display of silken flags of all the nations signatory to the Geneva Convention with the Stars and Stripes prominent among them. At the request of the Empress Augusta, who had ordered German women to make available samples of their cotton handiwork, Clara helped supervise setting up this German exhibit. She was a kind of patron and protector in the name of the Empress. The following spring Barton was back in Washington, where upon invitation she addressed the Conference of Charities and Correction. Time was less and less her own. The decision late in the year to close the house in Dansville is further evidence that she was being pulled in the direction of the corridors of power. Dansville had been a prized haven, and now she had little interest in being back in a place where often she had gone to recover her strength and repair her morale. She was prepared to sing Dansville's praises, telling a farewell gathering how "weak, worn, and tired, like a dog from the hunt, I have come back to it [Dansville] and to you, to lie down and lapse back into better strength, and go again."[20] But now she was going for the last time. Clara had become a star attraction on the American scene which had Washington as its stage.

For all of that Clara was not willing to forego field work should some catastrophe require her presence. Therein lay a serious problem bound to affect her future and that of the American Red Cross. It would dog her and in the end go a fair way toward explaining her final undoing as president of the national society. There were competing demands on her time and energy. If she continued to insist on being where the action was she could not but fail to build, or even to try to build, an infrastructure essential to the stability and orderly growth of the Red Cross in the United States. Whether on the road to deliver a series of talks or in the field face to face with disaster the effect on the Red Cross as an organization was the same. It lacked cohesion and direction. With advancing age she continued to think of "her child" as exactly that, her indisputable possession. By the late 1880s she should have concentrated her energies on administering her growing child. Then one thinks of her five months in Johnstown in the wake of the great flood of 1889, and realizes that there stood the true Clara Barton: charity in action. It was not in her nature to be a bureaucrat, even a top bureaucrat. She was instead a humanitarian, convinced that her high public profile was a necessary though secondary element— service in the field being primary—if the Red Cross was to go forward. For twenty years she insisted on being public property and private conscience, all the while neglecting the apparatus. Ultimately Barton fell between two stools. But in 1885 all this was locked in the recesses of future time. Thus when word was received of famine in Texas or a hurricane in South Carolina, Clara was prepared to drop everything in pursuit of service. The following list of natural and manmade troubles, each of which drew Barton like a magnet to join in the work of restoration is a graphic rendering of her commitment to pitch in personally, and not manage matters at a distance.

| | |
|---|---|
| 1885 – | Texas famine |
| 1886 – | Charleston earthquake |
| 1888 – | Tornado, Mount Vernon, Illinois |
| 1888 – | Florida yellow fever epidemic |
| 1889 – | Johnstown flood |
| 1892 – | Russian famine |
| 1893 – | South Carolina hurricane |
| 1894 – | Tidal wave on sea islands |
| 1896 – | Armenian massacres |
| 1897 – | Cuban relief for reconcentrados |
| 1898 – | Spanish-American War |
| 1900 – | Galveston storm and tidal wave |

Yet no mere list can begin to convey Clara Barton's full measure of devotion. Behind the list are a dozen stories. There were successes and failures worth recounting for an understanding of what the Red Cross became under Barton's sustained influence.

Emergencies calling for likely assistance from the Red Cross might be silent ones, the kind that fail to capture newspaper headlines. The Texas drought of 1885–1886 is a good example of slow rather than sudden death. It also exemplifies the caution that Barton was predisposed to exercise, even when aid from her society had been asked for. The difficulties in central and northwest Texas arose largely from a twenty-month drought that put a severe strain on the local population. A clergyman, John Brown of Albany, Texas, made a number of appeals for help by approaching Barton, among others. As he described the situation one hundred thousand families "were utterly destitute and on the verge of starvation."[21] Should this assessment be accurate it would well presage a calamity of major proportions. But had Brown provided exaggerated accounts? True, the governor of Texas had voiced appeals for food to care for those in need. In contrast many others believed the descriptions given by Brown nowhere matched the realities. The failure of the state legislature to take appropriate action on behalf of its own citizens appeared to underscore this position. Unwilling to admit defeat Brown came to Washington in January, 1885. When he met Clara Barton he had a simple request: come and see for yourself. Inasmuch as Grover Cleveland as president of the United States was Honorary Chairman of the American Red Cross Barton consulted him. He approved of the idea that Barton should indeed go to Texas and ascertain the facts. Accompanied by Dr. Hubbell, the two spent several days in the drought region. They found nothing like stark starvation, but the people there were "in the direst want of many necessities of life."[22] The region was edging toward a calamity. But was it a job for the Red Cross, or was it the responsibility of the state of Texas, once the extent of the dangers was made known to government officials. With these thoughts in mind Barton proceeded to Dallas. Colonel Belo, owner of the *Dallas News*, listened to her account of what she witnessed. He quickly agreed that the newspaper should be the voice alerting the state of the plight of those living in and around Albany. The state legislature was moved to vote $100,000 in relief money, with Colonel Belo making a personal contribution of $5,000. The Red Cross added modestly to the fund with Barton giving a small amount from her own purse. Furthermore she was very willing to lend her name in support of fund-raising from local private sources. At the same time she agreed with President Cleveland's veto of a congressional bill appropriating $10,000 to aid the distressed area. To her way of thinking the Texans must help themselves. More and more this was to become the stated position of the Red Cross under Barton's leadership. When people could help themselves they should not look to philanthropy, save to facilitate that self-help. Soon after Barton departed Texas the spring rains came enabling the farmers to look after the new crop and to save the surviving farm animals whose numbers had been severely reduced during the drought period. Though disappointed that the private fund-raising had been none too successful, Clara was firm in her conviction that God helps those who help themselves.

The American Amendment to the Geneva Convention was easier to state than it was to implement, as was well illustrated by the response of the Red Cross to the earthquake that struck Charleston, South Carolina, in August, 1886. Over the summer Barton had been visiting the western states, partly to vacation and partly to address and be honored at the fourth national convention of the Women's Welfare Corps meeting in San Francisco. On the return journey east, news of the Charleston quake broke. The city suffered heavy damage but Charlestonians, who were second to none in pride of place, were determined to rebuild the city. Organized and well supported by their neighbors they went quickly about their business. Barton decided she ought to visit the stricken area despite the limits on her time, energy, and resources. Except for her brief stay there it would be accurate to say that the Red Cross would have had no presence at all. As it was she distributed no more than $600 among several needy institutions, the bulk of the money supplied by the Chicago chapter. Upon returning to Washington arrangements were made to draw goods from the Red Cross warehouse to be sent to Charleston and given out by members of the Women's Relief Corps. There was no Red Cross flag to be seen. The insignificant response to the plight of Charleston combined with such efforts as were undertaken during the Texas "famine" underscore both the lack of a well-defined organizational purpose with a staff prepared to act with dispatch and a woeful want of operating funds. Clara Barton was still at the center of things. She would have welcomed the second of these propositions, namely, disposable funds in large amounts, but not at the price of yielding her leadership role. The Red Cross was hers! And perhaps the time was not fully ripe for abandoning the old ways. The Mount Vernon, Illinois, tornado that set down in February, 1888, and the ability of the Red Cross to come to the aid of the stricken populace was to be ample proof of this.

Clara's spirits had been buoyed up by her trip to Karlsruhe in the autumn of the year previous, there to attend the Fourth International Conference of the Red Cross. She again received a red-carpet welcome. Indeed a dazzling series of receptions, soirees, and dinners were much more a feature of this conference than serious Red Cross business. Meeting many of her old Swiss and German friends again, some of whom, such as Emperor Wilhelm I were major players in the European world of politics and diplomacy, was the kind of tonic Barton responded to. The prescription was a familiar one: praise without stint and a chance to please. From Karlsruhe she and Julian Hubbell went on to Paris and then London. It was mid-January before they arrived back in Washington.

The next month Mount Vernon, Illinois, was devastated. It took barely three minutes to destroy much of the town with a loss of thirty lives. Try as they might the people seemed unable to pull together to return the town to a level of livability. The growing feeling was that outside help was imperative, and it was to Clara Barton and the Red Cross that they turned. Barton replied quickly and acted effectively. Again Julian Hubbell did yeoman service. Upon entering Mount Vernon they were taken aback by the extent of the destruction. It was far greater than reports had indicated. Clara took command. She made sure the wire services reported on the severe conditions as she described them, and she entered a series of direct appeals for aid that were both touching and honest. The story hit a sensitive nerve in many communities once the news reached the surrounding areas and then penetrated faraway places. Donations came in almost unprecedented amounts. At the end of the day upwards of $90,000 in cash and bank drafts had been received. Barton not surprisingly, stressed the need for *things*, informing one donor that "nothing could be amiss . . . from bedsteads to a nutmeg grinder or a paper of pins."[23] For two weeks Barton and Hubbell and Enola Lee and John Morlan gave their all as they tended the sick, reopened a school, and organized teams of local citizens to be ready to take up where the Red Cross would leave off. Undoubtedly the drama of the tornado, so much sudden destruction, galvanized Clara's will to action. Once the initial cleanup had been accomplished Barton had no intention of remaining in Mount Vernon. The people there had been given both a jumpstart and direction. They must maintain the momentum thus supplied as the Red Cross pulled out. It had been only two weeks, but of intense activity, and Clara left the town with a deep sense of satisfaction. In her own mind no less than in that of the general public she had come through again. And she saw no reason to change her time-tested ways of relieving the hardships of the suffering.

In that same year, 1888, a yellow fever epidemic laid low Jacksonville, Florida. At first it appeared another opportunity for the Red Cross to demonstrate its unique capability in time of crisis. There is no question that the spread of the disease reached dangerous proportions. It is also true that the epidemic presented the Red Cross with problems not previously encountered. The most urgent need was for trained nurses who were likely to be immune to yellow fever. They could look after the sick and perhaps limit the spread of the fever. The sticking point in all this was the immunity requirement. Though dozens of nurses from the northern states were ready to volunteer to go south under the banner of the Red Cross, Barton would not authorize it. Nor did she visit Jacksonville itself for fear of infection. Instead she relied on the good offices of Colonel R. C. Southmayd, secretary of the New Orleans branch of the Red Cross. Southmayd was keen to help. He assembled some thirty nurses, white and black, male and female, recruited from the Old Howard Association, a local relief group. The feeling was that these southern-born individuals, perhaps at one time exposed to a mild form of the fever and who had recovered, were very likely to be immune.

Once in Florida and wearing the armband of the Red Cross as identity trouble quickly developed. Southmayd, a take-charge kind of man, quickly antagonized local officials, including the attending physicians, the very people who had been working to allay the spread of the sickness. Far worse, some of the nurses under Southmayd's direction were accused of drunkenness and a general neglect of their responsibilities. The *New York Herald*, with a taste for sensational journalism, gave wide coverage to these unfortunate incidents, to the detriment of the Red Cross's reputation.[24] Barton of course was thunderstruck but there was little she could do. As is often the case sensationalism sells while the good work done by many of the Red Cross nurses went unnoticed. At MacClenny, a town a distance from Jacksonville, ten nurses risked their lives as they left a moving train— no train would stop at MacClenny for fear of contagion—in order to minister to the many sick people there. On balance, however, the Red Cross lost more than it gained by way of public image, not a reassuring outcome for Clara who felt Southmayd had betrayed her.

More serious was the lesson the whole affair appeared to teach Barton. She had delegated authority to Colonel Southmayd, and however good were her intentions the results were a warning about the pitfalls of delegation. Clara was more convinced than ever that unless she were in the field and actively in charge of operations things could too easily go badly. In the short term this helps to explain why Barton was to be in the thick of things in the aftermath of the Johnstown flood the next year and why, no doubt, the Red Cross acquitted itself as it did. In the long term the results of the Jacksonville fiasco were more problematical. When years later pressure would build against her one-woman rule the evidence of her indispensability seemed to her overwhelming. The Red Cross without Clara Barton at the helm was unthinkable. It was difficult for her to see it any other way, or, to expect her to.

The Johnstown flood was an event of epic proportions, one that caught the eye and staggered the imagination of much of the nation. It has been equally fascinating to historians.[25] At the same time it stands out as providing the scene and setting for one of Clara Barton's finest hours. That may be claiming a lot but there are sound reasons for such a characterization. Unlike the Civil War, it made no strong, emotional, patriotic appeal. The later Spanish-American War brought back to Clara the romance and excitement of battle, something she thrived on, without much real danger of death. The wrecking of Johnstown, a coal and iron community in west central Pennsylvania, was prosaic by contrast. Then there were Barton's trips to Russia, to Armenia, with their exotic and recognizably historical overtones. At one point Clara would meet the czar of all the Russias! As for fires and floods and earthquakes and tidal waves, these were acts of nature over which men had no control. Johnstown was different from all the others. The flood was the result of carelessness and indifference on the part of a few, a flood that was attributable to human failure. It was a disaster that need not have happened, but it did. To use the length of the Red Cross's stay in Johnstown, upwards of five months, as a measuring stick, that alone places the flood relief undertaken as one of the most impressive Red Cross operations during the Barton years. Clara was not prepared to leave the region until she was confident Johnstown would rise from the wreckage.

To appreciate Clara Barton, the Red Cross, and Johnstown, it is best to follow closely Barton's own account. Reports coming out of the flood area were so startling and grim that both she and Dr. Hubbell, drawing on their considerable experience, sensed they were exaggerated. The loss of one thousand lives seemed unlikely for a town of thirty thousand inhabitants. The flood took three thousand lives, or about one-tenth of the population. What could people do facing a wall of water thirty feet high roaring down the narrow valley of the Conemaugh River? Families, as many as one hundred, were completely wiped out. Houses, barns, livery stables, banks, stores, schools all suffered the same fate. Property damage came to be estimated at more than ten million dollars.

Barton found it especially reprehensible that the flood was caused by the failure of the wall enclosing a huge manmade lake that held back the water. The artificial lake was fed by the Little Conemaugh River and had been created to provide a place of recreation for a group of wealthy Pittsburgh sportsmen. Heavy rains that May had saturated the ground, adding thousands of gallons of water to the weight putting pressure on earthen reinforcements. When the seventy-foot-high dam wall gave way, an event the down valley folks had long feared, the result was a "moving mountain of water."

Once news of the catastrophe reached Washington, Clara headed immediately for Johnstown. It took her five days to reach the site because of the prevailing chaos. What she saw and heard was enough to cow all but the heartiest. "I cannot lose the memory of that first walk on the first day," she told a gathering in Washington some months later. "The wading in the mud, the climbing over engines, cars, heaps of iron rollers, broken timbers, wrecks of houses, bent railway tracks, tangled piles of iron wire, bands of workmen, squads of military—the getting around the bodies of dead animals and often people being borne away. The smoldering fires and the drizzling rain."[26] Clara at once reported to General Hastings, Pennsylvania Militia commander; she explained who she was, her reason for being there and how she planned to help. Initially a bit skeptical Hastings nonetheless took Barton at her word. As far as he was concerned any assistance, amateur or professional, would be welcomed. Next Clara established a headquarters, a veritable command post, furnished from such debris as she found useful. In the field amenities were among her last concerns. She saw the need for things of all kinds by the thousands, for workers to set about the tasks of rebuilding, and for funds. The money raised was not for hand-outs but was to be used to buy supplies and tools. A warehouse was obtained to organize the materials as they arrived in response to her solicitations.

Although the weather was temperate that time of year, the great need and the greatest service performed by the Red Cross was the construction of living quarters. Lumber in goodly amounts had been donated by the people of Illinois and Iowa, specifically marked for the Red Cross. By the end of July the first of three large hotels was opened with two others soon to follow. The structures were simple, highly functional, and gave improved shelter to families who had been under tent or living in the open for weeks. Meanwhile the more familiar tasks of feeding the hungry, providing clothing for those without, distributing things of every description moved ahead. Under Barton's watchful eye the work of the Red Cross went smoothly to the satisfaction of all concerned from the Pennsylvania militia to the surviving town leaders. The results of all this effort prompted Clara to refer to it as "phenomenal and exceptional." Looking back at what she and her associates had accomplished in five months during which period aid of one kind or another was extended to some twenty thousand individuals Clara's assessment appears modest. She left it to others to sing the praises of the Red Cross. No one did it more eloquently or sincerely than Governor Beaver in a letter addressed to the people of Pennsylvania.

In this matter of sheltering the people, as in others of like importance, Miss Clara Barton, president of the Red Cross Association, was most helpful. At a time when there was a doubt if the Flood Commission could furnish houses of suitable character and with the requisite promptness, she offered to assume charge, and she erected with the funds of the association three large apartment houses which afforded comfortable lodgings for many houseless people. She was among the first to arrive on the scene of calamity, bringing with her Dr. Hubbell, the field officer of the Red Cross Association, and a staff of skilled assistants. She made her own organization for relief work in every form, disposing of the large resources under her control with such wisdom and tenderness that the charity of the Red Cross had no sting, and its recipients are not Miss Barton's dependents, but her friends.[27]

Most important for Clara, the Red Cross, still feeling humiliation because of press reports about irregularities in Jacksonville the previous year, was vindicated. This was duly noted by President Harrison upon Clara's return to Washington.

The American Amendment had provided for the peacetime activities of the Red Cross. What exactly it authorized however was a further and larger question. Wars, virtually by definition, are international in character but natural calamities may also have international ramifications. Clara Barton came face to face with the unresolved extent of the application of the Amendment during the Russian famine of the early 1890s. Should the American Red Cross concern itself with the suffering peasants of far-off Russia? An instinctive reaction could hardly be other than yes. A considered response could be otherwise. The German Red Cross had sent aid to the Mississippi flood victims. Could Americans do less for the unfortunate Russian farmers? For serious reasons, to be examined, the answer might go against involvement. Barton was not especially eager to volunteer her services. She was inclined to direct Red Cross aid only after it had been requested. The extent of the famine, some thirty million people were on the edge of starvation, meant that at the very best the Red Cross contribution would have a marginal impact. Then there were the political considerations, domestic and diplomatic. At the time Barton was continuing to battle to get official congressional recognition, that is, a federal charter for the Red Cross. From this all-important objective she did not want to be distracted. Apart from that there was the nature of the Russian government and for that matter the organization of its society. Both were inimical to American ideals. Russian autocracy was notorious for its repression of the masses which gave rise to doubts about the wisdom and propriety of helping such an antirepublican state. Aid given would merely perpetuate an evil system.

As compelling as such reservations were, not only to Barton but to Americans generally, the impulse to focus on the suffering of the people, while ignoring the political factors, was very strong. It was made so by the sheer numbers involved. The result was that several initiatives from various groups in New York and Philadelphia and in several midwestern farm states as well were taken to relieve the distress affecting so many of the Russian people. The Red Cross became one of several organizations to act, a reminder that its day as the major agency for providing emergency assistance was years distant.

The American Red Cross may have had little if any place in these relief efforts except for a request made of it by Benjamin Franklin Tillinghurst, editor of the Davenport, Iowa, *Democrat*. Enjoying an abundance of food and especially huge reserves of corn the people of the state, led by Governor Boies, enlisted in the cause of famine relief for Russia. The practical matter was how to get the grain from the source of plenty to the place of want. Enter Clara Barton. Tillinghurst knew Clara and admired her devotion to those who were down-and-out. He had given both Barton and the Red Cross favorable coverage in his newspaper. Once it became clear that the United States government would take no official action to provide shipping, Clara agreed to raise money to charter an oceangoing vessel, if the grain could be delivered to the port of New York. Pledges came in slowly but at last the $12,500 needed was in hand. The SS *Tynehead* was loaded with the contents of two hundred twenty-nine railroad cars. It sailed the first of May and arrived in Riga three weeks later, to be met there by Julian Hubbell who had come from Rome to see to the unloading and transshipment of the corn. He traveled into the countryside accompanied by Count Leo Tolstoi who as a lone individual had been attempting to care for the peasants living near his estate. Unfortunately for the many hungry people Hubbell encountered, the largesse he had on hand to distribute was small compared to other more ambitious undertakings. To put it in perspective, the American Red Cross supplied food to care for seven hundred thousand people for one month. New York and Philadelphia *ad hoc* associations provided much more. But by going international the American Red Cross had established and advanced an important precedent. Step by step Clara Barton demonstrated the credibility of her organization, and she was increasingly sure that one day Congress would extend to it a federal charter.

Barton's zeal and determination to make the Red Cross financially secure in one instance at least, caused her and the organization grave harm. Red Cross Park, nearly eight hundred acres of land near Bedford, Indiana, was deeded to Clara by Dr. Joseph Gardner in 1893. The deed named her rather than the Red Cross as the owner. It appeared the grandest of gifts. So much valuable land with standing timber, broad acres for crops, and a limestone quarry held the promise of income to support the Red Cross in action. Clara's imagination was fired by the prospects, particularly after she had visited the area, a fire stoked by Dr. Gardner who spoke of the possibility of a hospital or orphanage at the site. Both projects would be Red Cross sponsored. Why Dr. Gardner offered Clara this gift, though he admired her greatly, remains unclear, particularly so in light of ensuing events.

Someone was needed to administer the property. Barton chose John Morlan. He had served with her in Johnstown, and she judged him to be a young man of promise. In his short tenure as Park manager Morlan played her false. He expended considerable sums of Red Cross money, brought a dozen or so trotting horses and soon was entering his stable in local races. The money he won, and he won often, he kept as his own. To make matters worse, Morlan informed Clara that all the acreage had not actually been paid for, that $1,200 was due on a tract of eighty acres. Rather than give up the land, Barton paid off the debt from her own funds. It appears then that Dr. Gardner had also played her false. A disillusioning experience in itself, Red Cross Park was a ticking time bomb, later to be exploded and exploited by people wanting to cast doubts on Clara's integrity. The charge would be made that she had used her position as the head of the Red Cross as a means of personal profit through working the Park for its timber and limestone. Whatever Clara Barton lacked in accounting proficiency, a charge that she had gained financially is wholly unwarrantable.[28]

Death and destruction at Johnstown had been awesome. The devastation of the South Carolina Sea Islands in August, 1893, was more so. A hurricane with winds of overwhelming force struck the islands with such impact that an estimated five thousand people perished. Property damage was equally staggering. More than thirty thousand people had inhabited the land much of which became totally submerged. A breakdown of the whole social order ensued. Barton remembered the island well from her Civil War days spent there. She recalled the people as ordinary farmers and fishermen and mostly black. Believing the reports of damage as trustworthy, she concluded there was little the Red Cross could do with its slender resources. Only when Governor Benjamin Tillman of South Carolina asked her to visit the area and offer some assistance did Barton decide to see for herself what nature in its fury had wrought. Once there and having examined the state of social collapse it was not in Clara's nature to walk away. To her it became a test case for the reputation of the organization she had long directed in spite of the naysayers. "It is a perilous situation. If we fail we are lost," summed up her position.[29] The refusal both by the United States Congress and the South Carolina legislature (the latter in a shameless display of racism) to appropriate funds for a relief effort sharpened the challenge to the indomitable Red Cross chief. The desperate blacks were not to be left to fend for themselves. As one poor soul replied to the question how would he survive the answer was simple: to trust in God and Miss Barton.[30]

In conditions of extreme stress Barton could display a remarkable ability to put matters in perspective. The immediate need was food. So precious were supplies that a strict rationing plan was put into effect. It allowed daily one peck of hominy and a pound of pork for a family of seven. The allotment was increased for men who were working to rebuild dwellings and other necessary structures. Only the ill enjoyed tea, sugar, and bread in small quantities. In short the people had about enough food to sustain life. But survival was only phase one of Barton's overall plan to reverse the damage dealt by the hurricane.

To achieve that objective much help would have to be received from outside, and Barton sent out her familiar appeals for funds and for things. The response was not overly generous considering the severity of the damage. During a ten-month period about thirty thousand dollars in cash and goods valued at about thirty-five thousand dollars came in. Most of the offerings ranged from ten dollars to two-hundred fifty dollars. E. M. Wistar of Philadelphia gave ten thousand dollars, a gift that may well have spelled the difference between success and failure for the Red Cross on the Sea Islands. After food came clothing. A fair amount of old clothing reached the area, some of it fancy ball

gowns of the like that, at first glance, were hardly appropriate. Clara
set a group of women the task of cutting garments of all descriptions
for usage as well as for fit. She had done something like this at
Strasbourg back in 1871 and it was a lesson well learned. Waste not,
want not was a practice that came naturally to Clara. A third pressing
problem to be addressed was the spread of disease among the uprooted
population. Malaria and dysentery were commonplace and had to be
combatted. After some pressure exerted by friends in Washington, the
Treasury Department authorized two revenue cutters to ferry doctors
and medicine to isolated locales, there to drop off other supplies as
well. Before long the health of the community began to show improvement.

All these actions, and they were critical to survival, were preliminary to what Barton envisioned as the greater challenge, to rebuild the
Sea Island communities. She sought to ensure the long-term well-being of the people sorely abused by nature and government indifference. Eighteen ninety-four was the year of rebuilding. Lumber, tools,
and seeds were the main items required and after four months a
stockpile had been realized. It was then time to put them to use. The
long staple cotton industry was reestablished because Clara was able
to obtain the seeds. Houses were built from the five hundred thousand
feet of lumber purchased from the mainland. As good weather came
in the spring truck gardens began to flourish, providing almost
forgotten vegetables and fruit; chickens and hogs could be seen in
many yards. The bottom line was that hard work had paid off;
self-reliance was the key, befitting Barton's boast that the Red Cross
never made beggars out of people it helped.

Joel Chandler Harris, who was on the Sea Islands immediately after
the storm had passed, individually attempted to alleviate some of the
suffering among the people. He witnessed the Red Cross in action and
later wrote a touching tribute that appeared in *Scribner's Magazine* in
February, 1894. In part it read:

As a matter of fact, the Red Cross Society as I saw it at Beaufort is something
entirely different from any other relief organization that has come under my
observation. Its strongest and most admirable feature is its extreme simplicity.

The perfection of its machinery is shown by the apparent absence of all machinery. There are no exhibitions of self-importance. There is no display—no torturous cross-examination of applicants—no needless delay. And yet nothing is done blindly, or hastily, or indifferently. . . . Miss Barton and her assistants adopted from the very first the most rigid system of economy—a system far more efficacious in the end than any lavish dispensation of charity could have been.[31]

Contrast this with the conclusions offered by Sophia W. R. Williams in her article, "Miss Clara Barton and the Red Cross" published in *The Review of Reviews*, the very next month. Admitting that the Red Cross had been of great service to the suffering, the negative criticism offered stood out boldly as the following excerpt clearly indicates.

The National Red Cross Association in this country has been Miss Clara Barton, and Miss Clara has been the National Red Cross Society. . . . What the United States ought to have is a *National* Red Cross Society . . . with leading men in our great cities . . . on its board, with delegates from the Philadelphia College of Physicians and Surgeons, and the New York Academy of Medicine . . . and the Army, Navy, and Marine Hospital Staff, on its board of surgical and medical control and with a constituency representing the entire country. Instead the country has Miss Clara Barton.

But when one asks for detailed reports, for itemized statements of disbursements, for a careful recapitulation of its labors, its achievements, its failures, its experience and the teaching and lesson of its work—these things either do not exist or are not furnished. . . . I asked its officers for reports. I pleaded for all of its statements and two or three pamphlets were all I could secure. Manifestly these things ought not to be. This national body ought to have a national organization, a national board, and reports which would stand as model and guide for all relief work, the country over.[32]

Oddly enough these two estimates are not totally inconsistent because each author was focusing on different aspects of their common subject. No one, then or now, could deny the "great service to humanity" offered by Clara Barton. Harris saw it at first hand and marveled at it because of the very lack of machinery. It was the absence of a mechanism that troubled Williams, and she committed to print what a growing number of people had been thinking. To some extent aware of the need for machinery Barton usually expressed this in terms of having leading figures from the world of business and philanthropy as members of the Red Cross Board. Men who would give large sums of money would encourage many others to do likewise. But depersonalizing the Red Cross, separating her from it in any way she continued to believe was beside the point. The point was more money. Clara could and would take it from there.

Criticisms leveled at the Red Cross offended Clara Barton; they did not deter her. They did, however, make her more conscious of the negative effects of public and private opinion. In consequence she became more cautious in her response to calls for aid when fresh disasters struck. The world being the world there was no want of human misery crying out for amelioration. A massacre of Armenians by the armies of the Ottoman Empire was one such struggle that caught America's attention, one that eventually drew Barton into committing the American Red Cross in another faraway clime. The smoldering hostility between Turk and Armenian, between Muslim and Christian, flared up once more in the mid-1890s when the Armenians sought to establish an independent state. This attempt was put down with draconian measures by the militarily superior Turks who resorted to a scorched-earth policy to deracinate their enemies— men, women, and children. There were American missionaries in Armenia at the time, and news of atrocities was soon being reported regularly by the American press. These reports were greeted by a rising tide of anger.

A National Armenian Relief Committee, composed of important public and private men, was set up in New York City. It recognized that what it needed was an agent to travel to Armenia and get on with the job of saving the people from further anguish. A professed Christian organization would not do. The Ottomans would interpret this as a hostile move, designed to aid the Armenian rebels at Turkish expense. Only a strictly neutral body would have any hope of success, and even that would depend on the willingness of the Turks to allow it to enter their country. Despite doubts about the ability of the Red Cross and its leadership, it was the obvious and only answer of solving the committee's dilemma. Spencer Trask, a leading committee member, approached Clara Barton. He held forth the prospect of large sums of money along with the promise of full support. Barton hesitated. It appeared to her unlikely that the Sultan would agree to a foreign intrusion. Clara was still smarting from the abuse she had taken in the public prints after the Sea Islands operation. Why, after all, did she make the commitment asked of her by Trask? Certainly the prospect of helping people as badly treated as the Armenians had a strong appeal. Helping people was her mission in life. At the same time it provided a fresh opportunity to demonstrate the range, dedication and know-how of the Red Cross. She would silence her critics and magnify the importance of the Red Cross with the same stroke.

In late January, 1896, Barton and a small staff headed by Julian Hubbell set sail for the Old World once again. Held up in London awaiting Sultan Abdul-Hamid II's permission to enter any part of his domain Clara trusted Alexander Terrell, the United States minister to the Sublime Porte, to clear the way. Terrell was successful in arranging for Barton to speak with important Turkish officials. Coming on to Constantinople in mid-February she was granted an audience with Tewfik Pasha. She reminded him that though Christian she was bound by the Geneva Convention (to which the Ottomans were a signatory) to aid all those in distress, irrespective of religion or nationality. A somewhat disingenuous argument since the overwhelming majority of those in need of assistance, about three hundred and fifty thousand people, were Armenian Christians, it appeared to reassure Tewfik. Her only purpose in being there she said was to give out food and medicine. But Tewfik also had a card to play. Yes, he would permit Barton to supervise the aid she would arrange for, but it must be done in her name, and not in the name of any New York committee, or even that of the Red Cross. She had no counterstroke, and with a growing awareness of how desperate the fate of the Armenians was daily becoming she agreed. How this might look from the perspective of

New York did not greatly worry her. What did worry her was how soon she could get her staff out into the field.

In Turkey Clara herself decided to remain in the capital city. The rugged terrain, the great distances to travel with primitive transport, the physical dangers combined to persuade this seventy-five-year-old lady to remain in Constantinople. Her work was administrative: procurement of supplies, bartering for bargains to stretch her funds, currency exchange, correspondence and perhaps transcending such activities, a presence in the thinking of the Ottoman authorities whose distrust of Barton's associates was apparent.

Things in the field ran, if not smoothly, at least satisfactorily. Relations between Barton and the New York Committee deteriorated. Her sponsors resented the fact that it was Barton who was gaining credit for the enterprise rather than either the Red Cross or themselves. But if the charge were true that Clara Barton was the Red Cross and the Red Cross was Clara Barton it was a gratuitous objection to make. For its part the committee never delivered the huge sums of money it had promised, the final amount collected being $116,000. A late donation of five thousand dollars was given to the Home Missionary Society which continued its work in Armenia. Exasperated by the carping of the New York people at one stage, Clara declared: "We will finish the job without further aid."[33]

Altogether five separate expeditions went into the hinterland. They were escorted by Turkish authorities without whose protection little could have been accomplished. Food was delivered, medicine made available, and a faint ray of hope enkindled. With uncertain means and a small staff Clara Barton and/or the Red Cross acquitted itself admirably. One unexpected result of the Americans in Armenia was improvement in Turco-American diplomatic relations. Clara had been something of an ambassador of good will, and she was properly honored by citations and medals presented her by the Ottoman government.

Atrocities much closer to home were soon raising fresh hackles on the American conscience. The proposition that the United States, in Jefferson's oft-quoted phrase: "America, the world's last, best hope," was giving off a new resonance as the nineteenth century closed. With the coming of the new century, what would become the American century, Jefferson's rhetoric many would have translated into positive meaning. The new understanding of the hoary phrase had it that the United States, given its power and purpose, should begin to police in an active way the whole of the Western Hemisphere. President Cleveland's abrupt 1895 notice to Great Britain to back off in its boundary dispute with Venezuela attested to this altered attitude. The real test was to come in Cuba. The largest island of the Caribbean, it lay a scant ninety miles off the United States mainland. Nationalism that had spread across Latin America beginning early in the century had come to Cuba no less than to other parts of the dying Spanish Empire. It gave rise to the cry: Cuba for Cubans, Cuba libre. The Spanish mother country seemed determined to retain its hold on the island, the last vestige of Spanish imperialism in the New World. By resort to extreme measures of military repression and reprisal it proposed to stamp out the Cuban spirit of independence which had manifested itself by armed insurrection. One of the methods used was termed reconcentration. Since portions of the population supported the insurrectos, either openly or secretly, the Spanish generals sought to cut away this backing by herding large numbers of Cubans into reconcentration camps, a form of reverse no-go zones. This was designed to deny the armed Cuban nationals their base of support. Camp living conditions quickly became deplorable. Due to shortages of food and water and without access to medical attention, the camps were a form of enslavement. Brutal treatment and plain neglect typified the camps, and tales of misery and abuse soon reached America. There was a growing feeling that the United States must do something to relieve if not eliminate such sordid conditions. People ready to promote American action approached Clara Barton to seek her advice and possible assistance. By this time Barton was wary of involving the Red Cross outside the nation. She was willing to listen to these Cuban relief enthusiasts, and just possibly to cooperate with them.

The first people to come Barton's way, a contingent she would term "the court ladies," were the wives of prominent Washingtonians in

and out of government. They styled their group the National Relief
Fund for the Aid of Cuba. Viewed one way they made up a band of
simple, perhaps naive, do-gooders without the faintest conception of
what was involved in relief work. But Clara, as often was the case with
her, wondered if perhaps there was an ulterior motive on their part in
seeking her advice. Were they trying to use the name of the Red Cross
to their own advantage? Fearing the worst Barton was able to arrange
a meeting with President McKinley. She wanted to sound him out on
official government policy with respect to Cuba and what if any part
the Red Cross might be expected to have in the event help would be
forthcoming. By drawing on her recent experience with the Ottoman
government she was especially conscious of the need to obtain Spanish
authorization for aid to be given the reconcentrados. Precipitous
moves by Americans could only be construed by Madrid as unfriendly.
At this point the McKinley administration had little desire to provoke
Spain though it was coming under increasing public pressure to "do
something" about conditions in Cuba. The cautious McKinley responded to Clara's implied wish to have the Red Cross be *the* American
relief agency, should it come to that, by promising to take the whole
matter under advisement.

Pursuant to discussions with Barton, the secretaries of state, war
and navy, and private citizens interested in seeing that action be taken,
the president announced the establishment of the Central Cuban
Relief Committee. Its purpose was to raise funds and gather quantities
of food, medicine, and other necessities. A committee of three included Stephen E. Barton, Clara's nephew Steve, Louis Klopisch of
the *Christian Herald,* and Charles Schieren, an influential New Yorker.
Meanwhile Barton had been in communication with the Spanish
minister to Washington, Depuy de Lome, to inquire about the
likelihood that his government would permit a relief expedition to
reach the suffering people of Cuba. As matters stood at the end of
1897, all this added up to a delicately balanced set of circumstances.
The delivery of a large amount of assistance could help frustrate the
Spanish effort to keep Cuba in line. American actions could well be
construed as meddling in the internal affairs of Spain. If there was any

way to defuse this potentially explosive situation, it would be the presence of the International Red Cross on the island, supervising the distribution of food, clothing, and medicine in accordance with the Geneva Convention, of which Spain was a signatory power. The American Red Cross agents in the field would be there to serve humanity, whether it meant feeding a malnourished reconcentrado or a sick or wounded Spanish soldier. It must be said that the American people were concerned with aiding the Cubans, and not ministering to Spanish soldiery. This created a dilemma for the American Red Cross from the outset of the relief plan's implementation. The horns of the dilemma were sharpened by the sinking of the USS *Maine* in February, 1898, and even more so by the declaration of war in April. From the beginning it was the desire and intention of the American people to relieve the Cubans, the victims of Spanish repression. Spain was the villain in their eyes and villains deserved only contempt. They should not be the beneficiaries of American generosity. No one recognized the perils of the situation more acutely than Clara Barton. It preyed on her mind as she arrived in Havana on February 9. The United States and Spain were at peace, and it was hoped they could remain so. A week later and only two days after Clara had dined aboard the *Maine* the battleship was sunk as it rode anchor in Havana harbor with a loss of two hundred sixty officers and other ranks. America exploded. "Remember the Maine, To Hell with Spain" bellowed the newspapers. Despite the best efforts of the American minister to Madrid, Stewart L. Woodford, President McKinley succumbed to what he interpreted as the popular will. The United States and Spain were at war.

Perhaps the war could not have been avoided after all. The condition of the Cuban people, as Barton quickly discovered, was indeed desperate. "The massacres of Armenia seemed merciful in comparison," she wrote, especially as concerned women and children.[34] A nation can sit on the horns of a dilemma only so long. At the time Woodford was exercising all his diplomatic skills in Madrid to prevent the war, Barton was verifying the horror stories that had been appearing in the American press for months. Until war was officially declared she was free to go about the island to give what aid and comfort she could; in her mind politics had no place when it came to helping the needy. Senator Redfield Proctor, a Vermont Republican and a politician of considerable influence, came to see for himself. Clara acted as his guide and source of information. He too was appalled by what he saw and told the American people so when he reported back to his Senate colleagues. Proctor was much impressed by Barton and the Red Cross, having nothing but praise for the methods being used to assist the population. Clara would find this kind of statement valuable because she was to have critics as well. The chief among them was Louis Klopisch of the Relief Committee. He came to Cuba and roundly scored the Red Cross for the red tape he contended he encountered. Barton became so exasperated with him that she left Cuba to return to Washington determined to have a final, official statement defining the relationship between the Relief Committee and the Red Cross. She got what she wanted. President McKinley reaffirmed the previous understanding: the committee would raise funds and provide goods and the Red Cross would be solely responsible for the distribution.

Sensing that the war could not be far off, in April Barton chartered the SS *State of Texas* for the purpose of conveying all available supplies to Cuba. The declaration of war came before the ship was able to sail for Cuba and land its cargo. With Cuba now under blockade the ranking naval officer, Admiral Willis T. Simpson, refused permission for the *State of Texas* to enter Cuban waters. His reasoning was sound from a military point of view. Food and medicine delivered by the Red Cross in good faith could easily be seized by the Spanish army. The net effect would be to aid the enemy and this the navy could not allow. Other problems developed. The army was not prepared to allow the Red Cross to operate on the field of battle. The McKinley administration had announced in June that the Red Cross was authorized free passage in the war zone but field commanders considered the organization meddlesome at best and a likely obstacle to military operations. Barton was beginning to think that she received more cooperation from the Turkish officers than from those of her own country.

Events rather than plans determined the outcome of the mission of Barton, the Red Cross, and the *State of Texas*. When the United States fleet moved to engage the enemy at Santiago the *State of Texas* made land nearby. It moored at Siboney, ready to help and was of almost immediate assistance to troops wounded in the skirmish fighting. In this setting Clara Barton was her old Civil War self. The similarities however could be discouraging as well as energizing. The Army Medical Service was unprepared even to the basic needs: cots, blankets, sufficiency of medicine. Unlike the Civil War, the Red Cross was there to make up for these deficiencies. The army surgeons grudgingly accepted this help because only the Red Cross was able to supply their needs. Gradually the army came to see the Red Cross not as an intruder but as a friend. By early July, after the heavy fighting at El Caney and San Juan Hill, Red Cross doctors, including Hubbell and Gardner (with whom Clara had been reconciled) were working side by side with the military surgeons. Barton's comment on the sequence of events leading up to the cooperation between the military and civilian medical teams is worth notice. "If we could have been permitted or properly called to the field only a month before the outbreak there would have been no unnecessary suffering, no lack of food, or care, or nurses."[35]

Expediency had had its effect as the resistance of the army doctors to the presence of Red Cross workers softened. In one particular way, however, the army stuck to its guns. The surgeon general, George M. Sternberg, was utterly opposed to female nurses, despite the need of them and the willingness of the Red Cross, with the assistance of the Central Cuban Relief Committee, to provide them. But again events tended to shape outcomes. With the spread of malaria, typhoid, and yellow fever, this refusal to make use of the skills of several hundred trained nurses who had volunteered their service was foolhardy. At last, and at most, Sternberg agreed to allow women to work on hospital ships and in army hospitals stateside, but not in field hospitals. It amounted to a limited victory both for Barton and the cause of female emancipation.

With the war progressing favorably for the United States, Barton decided to take the *State of Texas* from Siboney to Santiago, a judgment based in large part on her belief that the civilians of the region were in desperate straits. Admiral Simpson in a rare show of approval of the work of the Red Cross allowed the *State of Texas* to lead the fleet as it entered Santiago harbor. "Miss Barton was standing on the forward deck. A hundred glasses were trained on her as she stood queenly and majestic, one of the bravest of the brave, always going where suffering humanity needed her most," wrote one eyewitness."[36] For Clara this was no time for posturing heroics. There were people to feed, sickness to treat, wounds to heal. Within days of arrival at Santiago thousands had been fed and clothed and in keeping with the letter and spirit of the Geneva Convention, civilian and soldier alike. Colonel Theodore Roosevelt, commanding officer of the first United States Volunteer Cavalry, was among them. The story of his first encounter with the Red Cross in Cuba in 1898 has had different versions told. The heart of the matter is not in dispute. Hearing that a Red Cross station was near his exhausted troopers, Roosevelt came upon Barton and Dr. Gardner as they were about their work. He asked if he could buy some delicacies: malted milk, canned fruit, chocolate. He was informed they were not for sale. When Roosevelt persisted, as was his wont, he was told that though the items were not for sale he could have what he chose simply by asking. Greatly relieved and pleased the future president filled a large sack with as much as he could carry, slung it over his shoulder, and with a cordial thank you strode off in the direction of the Rough Riders encampment.[37]

At the end of August the Red Cross unit moved from Santiago to Havana. The fighting was all but over. At Havana the Spanish officials—the city had not yet formally surrendered—were still in charge. The Red Cross ship was required to pay a fee of $500 for permission to enter the harbor. This Barton was willing to do but she refused to begin any off-loading of supplies when informed that all such material would be under Spanish control. The decision was then taken to leave Cuba for home. Knowing that there was much more work to be done in Cuba in the coming months she planned to return.

## NOTES

1. Foster Rhea Dulles, *The American Red Cross: A History*, New York: Harper and Brothers, 1950, p. 19.

2. Clara Barton, *A Story of the Red Cross*, New York: Airmont Publishing Company, Inc., 1968, is basic to this chapter.

3. Elizabeth B. Pryor, *Clara Barton Professional Angel*, Philadelphia: University of Pennsylvania Press, 1981, p. 208.

4. Barton to Hamilton Fish, March 4, 1883, Clara Barton *Papers*, Library of Congress.

5. Ishbel Ross, *Clara Barton: Angel of the Battlefield*, Indianapolis: Bobbs Merrill, 1949, p. 281.

6. William E. Barton, *The Life of Clara Barton*, 2 vols., New York: AMS Press, 1969, vol. 2, p. 207.

7. Ibid., p. 208.

8. Ibid., p. 212.

9. Ibid., pp. 212–13.

10. Ross, *Angel of the Battlefield*, p. 154.

11. Blanche C. Williams, *Clara Barton: Daughter of Destiny*, Philadelphia: J. P. Lippincott Company, 1941, p. 284.

12. Pryor, *Professional Angel*, pp. 197–98.

13. Ross, *Angel of the Battlefield*, p. 156.

14. Pryor, *Professional Angel*, p. 234.

15. Ross, *Angel of the Battlefield*, p. 156.

16. Barton to A. S. Solomons, March 7, 1884, Clara Barton *Papers*.

17. Ross, *Angel of the Battlefield*, p. 157.

18. Joseph Sheldon to Julian Hubbell, Oct. 13, 1884, Clara Barton *Papers*.

19. Pryor, *Professional Angel*, pp. 238–39.

20. Williams, *Daughter of Destiny*, p. 294.

21. William Barton, *The Life of Clara Barton*, vol. 2, p. 224.

22. Ibid., p. 226

23. Barton to Robert Princhard, March 6, 1888, Clara Barton *Papers*.

24. Pryor, *Professional Angel*, p. 256.

25. David McCullough, *The Johnstown Flood*, New York: Simon and Schuster, 1968, is the most authoritative account.

26. Barton, Letter Book, Clara Barton *Papers*.

27. William Barton, *The Life of Clara Barton*, vol. 2, p. 236.

28. Pryor, *Professional Angel*, pp. 272–75; pp. 288–89 has a full account.

29. Dulles, *The American Red Cross: A History*, p. 33.

30. Williams, *Daughter of Destiny*, p. 332.

31. Joel Chandler Harris, "The Sea Islands Hurricane: The Relief of the Sea Islands," *Scribner's Magazine*, v. 15, n. 3, March, 1894, p. 270.

32. Sophie Williams, "Miss Barton and the Red Cross," *The Review of Reviews*, v. 9, n. 50, March, 1894, p. 315.

33. Pryor, *Professional Angel*, p. 294.

34. Dulles, *The American Red Cross: A History*, p. 44.

35. Barton to Sir Vincent Barrington, Aug. 24, 1898, Clara Barton *Papers*.

36. Pryor, *Professional Angel*, p. 314.

37. In Roosevelt's *The Rough Riders* the Red Cross is mentioned but four times and then only in passing. Barton's name is cited once but there is no description of the meeting of Roosevelt and Barton as Barton has described it. *The Works of Theodore Roosevelt*, 24 volumes, New York: Charles Scribner's Sons, 1924, *The Rough Riders*, vol. 13, pp. 3–361.

# ——6——

# *Road to Rejection*

Through the years Clara Barton directed the Red Cross and its operations she sometimes thought that only a war could cement the National Association into place in the hearts and minds of the American people. Then came the Spanish-American conflict which, in her theorizing, should have provided the requisite conditions for the final triumph of her organization. Instead the opposite occurred. Criticism of the conduct of the Red Cross in Cuba centered on Barton and on her methods. The road to rejection began in Cuba, and the journey along it would be long and painful arriving at the end with Clara's forced resignation in 1904. The wartime Red Cross carried with it the seeds of its own demise, the end of the association as Barton had shaped it and in some sense the destruction of Clara in her life's work if not in legend. She did not surrender easily, or willingly, or happily. The stone that was the foundation stone was rejected by the builders.

By the 1890s the managerial revolution in the American corporate world was well advanced. "The visible hand of management replaced the invisible hand of market mechanisms," in the words of Alfred D. Chandler.[1] Something akin to this change was taking place in other institutions, in the prominent universities, for example. It was no longer a matter of challenge and response, but of mapping out the direction that such institutions would take according to well-conceived plans. Applying this business principle to the Red Cross, it is appropriate to say that the whole idea of a relief agency had grown so imposing in the public consciousness it could no longer remain a matter of response to successive crises. Rather, reflexive action must be replaced by the visible hand of management with its permanent and centralized methods of control, supported by a trained and competent staff and able to draw on significant reliable financing. The amateur was to give way to the professional.

Clara Barton's insistence on keeping in place her understanding of what the Red Cross should be and how it was to function was running against a swift tide of change. Nothing symbolized this better than her house at Glen Echo, Maryland. In 1890 two brothers, Edwin and Edward Baltzley, had purchased a large tract of land at Glen Echo, some miles northwest of Washington. They envisioned a planned community, designed to appeal to the well-off and the well educated. Believing that an association with the Red Cross would add prestige to their development, the Baltzleys offered Clara a parcel of land and agreed to help build her a house. She accepted the proposal and construction was soon underway. Due to various delays Barton did not fully occupy the premises until 1897. What she got in the bargain was an imposing frame building, much too large for a residence but, Clara judged, a structure quite suitable to be both her home and the headquarters of the American Red Cross. Looking at the house today, for it still stands and is maintained by the National Park Service, it comes across as a metaphor of Barton's persistent belief that the old ways were best, or to phrase it differently, of her rejection of the visible hand of management. The first floor consisted of a parlor and reception room, connected by a wide hallway to a dining room and kitchen along with office space for Barton and three or more assistants. The center hall was made wide enough to provide built-in cupboards, there to store supplies the Red Cross could quickly call upon in case of emergencies. The second floor provided sleeping quarters for Clara and her small staff, and a third floor could be used for both sleeping and storage. It was a residence, a headquarters, and a warehouse all in one! Well suited no doubt for the needs of the Red Cross when it was launched, by 1900 Glen Echo was anachronistic. The Clara Barton House is a reminder that not only individuals from Mabel Boardman to Theodore Roosevelt would act to make the Red Cross into a different and more viable institution but of the large forces changing the way America organized its giant corporations, and as it turned out, the way it would dispense its charity. In the new age of efficiency through new organizational methods neither Clara Barton nor the house at Glen Echo was to have a place.

Upon Barton's return to the United States at the end of the Spanish-American War indications surfaced that the old ways must give ground. The New York Red Cross, responding to a basic organizational principle that held that power will seek to fill a vacuum, appeared poised to supersede the national association in importance. The New Yorkers had performed yeoman service during the war and came to be looked upon, in some quarters at least, as the most dynamic component of the American Red Cross. This threat of takeover, whether real or imagined, Barton feared and resented. Paranoia such as she had frequently exhibited in the past again dominated her outlook. Another source of worry that appeared dangerous was the attitude of the military toward her. The Army Medical Service had been embarrassed by an inability to respond to the needs of men in the field and was still smarting from the impression given that it had been upstaged by a little old lady when it came to caring for the sick and wounded soldiers. Fortunately for Clara President McKinley's admiration and friendship momentarily protected her from adverse army moves. That could change should he leave office in 1901. Scattered opposition to Barton was based on her age; she was seventy-six when she went to war in 1898. It was a criticism Clara brushed aside, but the fact was she was getting older day by day!

The terms of the Peace of Paris (1898) formally ending the Spanish-American War brought the United States an empire, explicitly and implicitly, in the Far East and in the Caribbean. The Philippines and Puerto Rico became American possessions and Cuba, freed from Spain, was an informal protectorate. American troops were to stay in Cuba until 1902 (and to return in 1906) as the political leadership sought to create the mechanism for a self-governing nation and animate the spirit that would enable it to succeed. The immediate plight of the mass of Cubans was another matter, not directly affected by the efforts afoot to achieve political stability. The condition of the people, especially in the rural areas, was desperate and steps had to be taken at once to alleviate their suffering. Not surprisingly President McKinley extended to the National Red Cross, as distinct from the New York branch, official permission to take up the tasks, including the supervision of hospitals and orphanages. Economic recovery initiatives were not part of the mandate however. The question remained, what specific part would Clara Barton have in the work of rehabilitation? Lacking a dramatic crisis Clara at first was prepared to stay in Washington and direct operations from there. The field agents were led by Dr. Hubbell in whom Barton continued to have the utmost confidence. After several weeks Barton decided she must go back to Cuba and superintend the work being done, even though she had no cause to complain about the conduct of Hubbell and the team of agents. Even Hubbell came to resent Clara's presence, the implication being that Barton no longer trusted his judgment. Loss of confidence in Hubbell is a good indication of how deep Barton's paranoia went. Adding to the growing tension was her fear that the New York Red Cross was about to make a power grab. She decided the way to thwart such a move was to pull out the American Red Cross altogether, leaving relief work in Cuba to the army and a hastily organized Cuban Red Cross chapter.[2] Barton's state of mind by this time, midsummer, 1899, was extremely unsettled. Despite efforts of nephew Stevé to persuade her that the New Yorkers planned no *coup* she could not be convinced.[3] She badly needed some assurance that the national body would continue to be the unchallenged center of Red Cross activities. Lacking that Barton might not be able to carry on.

Barton's passage down the road of rejection was not one of uninterrupted distress and discouragement. The year 1900 indicated that, and for good reason. The long-sought incorporation of the American National Red Cross by an act of Congress came in June when President

McKinley signed the bill into law.[4] No doubt the Spanish-American War had placed the Red Cross in a favorable light, the negative criticisms far outweighed by the praise of soldiers, newspapers, and the general public. The fight for incorporation had been a prolonged one with uncertainty as to the outcome almost to the last. Clara was more exhausted than elated by official approval. And even this victory had a down side, namely, the requirement that the War Department make an annual audit of the Red Cross account books. Though there was nothing of an ethical nature to fear in this regard because money and supplies received were always put to good use, when it came to strict procedures auditors might well find what, as professionals, they would deem irregularities. Clara had continued to be cavalier when it came to keeping records of the receipt and disbursement of funds. She always insisted that what she did was in response to need, which was the essence of her work, and not with an eye to the judgment of auditors. She was content to allow others to "regularize" the record. The law of incorporation further required a number of new operating rules, including the election of officers who would be responsible to a new Board of Control. Barton was satisfied that under the 1900 law the Red Cross, as it came from her hand, was now situated to grow in numbers and in strength. In consequence she offered to step down as president and to allow another to take charge of directing future growth. Soon to be seventy-nine she appeared to realize her limitations for leading the Red Cross into a new age. Instead she was re-elected president in what was to be one of the crueler ironies of her life. Flattered by what had occurred, she convinced herself that perhaps one more year of leadership would be best for all concerned.[5]

Three months later, as though to test the wisdom of her resolve to stay on, Galveston, Texas, was nearly destroyed by a hurricane and resulting tidal wave. It was Johnstown and the Sea Islands combined. Upwards of six thousand people perished and property damage ran into the millions. Barton reported the extent of the disaster in telling phrase.

Here again no description could adequately serve its purpose. The sea, with fury spent, had sullenly retired. The strongest buildings, half standing, roofless and tottering, told what once had been the make-up of a thriving city. But that cordon of wreckage skirting the shore for miles it seemed, often twenty feet in height, and against which the high tide still lapped and rolled! What did it tell? The tale is all too dreadful to recall—the funeral pyre of at least five thousand human beings. The uncoffined dead of the fifth part of a city lay there. The lifeless bodies festering in the glaring heat of a September sun told only too fatally what that meant to that portion of the city left alive. The streets were well-nigh impassable, the animals largely drowned, the working force of men diminished, dazed, and homeless. The men who had been the fathers of the city, its business and its wealth, looked on aghast at their overwhelmed possessions, ruined homes, and, worse than all, mourned their own dead.[6]

What could the Red Cross do, and what would Clara do in light of her increasingly worn condition? To offer advice to the field agents, to be active in raising relief funds, and to husband her strength—all this could have been accomplished by remaining in Washington. But once the call came from Galveston asking the Red Cross to step in, Barton's decision to go personally to the devastated city was a matter of conditioned response. She confided to her journal: "It was naturally my work to go."[7] The offer of the *New York World* to help raise funds that the Red Cross in turn would dispense simply confirmed Clara in her decision. Some members of the Board of Control, notably Ellen Spencer Mussey the elected vice president, had reservations about Clara making the trip, one which was to take five days by train, but Barton was too practiced in doing what she chose to do to heed such advice.

The pattern of the Red Cross efforts in Galveston was a familiar one, but somewhat abbreviated. Barton and her team stayed only two months before heading back to Washington. Meanwhile she had been once again in her element: directing the field agents, arranging for construction of shelters, seeing to the distribution of food, clothing, and medicine. Only about one hundred twenty thousand dollars was raised by and for the Red Cross, a truly small sum given the extent of death and damage and the costs of rebuilding. The city fathers nonetheless valued the efforts of the Red Cross, declaring that the mere presence of Clara Barton among them had given them the determination to pick up the pieces and render Galveston a livable place once again.[8] With a flair for the spectacular Barton, on her departure, arranged to supply a million strawberry plants to replace the crop the storm had destroyed. The farmers to their delight and profit were able to harvest a crop that became a symbol of hope reborn.

Upon returning to Washington Barton came face to face with something she had never before encountered. According to the by-laws under incorporation she must submit a report of the Red Cross activities in Galveston. One of the requirements that Congress had set down was an accounting of all funds received and disbursed. Tension between Barton and the board quickly surfaced with seeds of latter-day friction amply sown. To Clara the board's implementation of this provision was petty, if not calculated to embarrass her. To the board Clara's resentment of any request for information was a sign of her questionable fitness for the Red Cross presidency.

The road to rejection had again turned rocky and realizing this Clara decided on a bold move. At the annual meeting of the association in December, 1901, she sought a change in the by-laws. This included the abolition of the Board of Control, to be replaced by a Board of Directors to which the president would not have to be so strictly accountable. Such was her personal popularity that her proposal was approved. It was a Pyrrhic victory. The problems of person and methods, the causes of the strain between Clara and the Board of Control, had not thereby disappeared. In the coming months they were in truth to become exacerbated. Moving the Red Cross headquarters to Manhattan, intended to give Barton access to the big money in New York City, failed in its purpose. Familiar with the ways and means of Washington dating back to Civil War days, Clara was uncomfortable and ineffectual in winning the support of moneyed New Yorkers. To many observers and to an increasing number of interested parties the Red Cross once again appeared to be adrift.

Attendance at the Seventh International Red Cross Conference held at St. Petersburg in the late spring of 1902 gave Barton the opportunity to show, despite appearances, that she was still the personification of the Red Cross in America. It was to be "her last flash of glory."9 The manner in which she was greeted and the esteem in which she was held may have been disconcerting to other members of the American delegation, especially to Ellen Mussey who by this time had become one of Clara's harshest critics. But to Barton the adulation of the Europeans was nothing new so that her sedate and gracious acknowledgment of popularity only added to her reputation as a great lady. Barton had often lamented that prominent Americans rarely treated her with the high regard displayed by the crowned heads in the Old World. She felt she truly was a prophet without honor at home. That both puzzled and saddened her. In St. Petersburg and Moscow, in Berlin and of course Karlsruhe, in these great cities, she came as an American queen. Czar Nicholas was particularly attentive. Along with other delegations the Americans were presented to Nicholas and Alexandra at Tsarkoe Selo. Clara was much impressed by the young couple and their obvious affection for one another. The day after the presentation the Court Chamberlain bestowed on Clara the "Decoration of the Empire" in the name of the Czar.10 She alone among all the delegates was so honored.

The conference gathering itself was a chance to meet with old friends and here, as well as in the palace precincts, Clara was acclaimed. She was much impressed by how well organized and fully supported many of the European national societies were, in sharp contrast to her American experience where funds had to be coaxed from the public. She wrote of this to Mrs. John A. Logan, one of her warmest friends within the ranks of the American Red Cross. "We in the U.S. do not know much of the splendid Red Cross organizations of the Old World with their armies of numbers, their resources in treasure and equipment, and their preparedness for calls to duty."11 How, Clara might have thought, had she failed to accomplish the same at home.

Nowhere was she to receive as warm and loving a welcome as at Karlsruhe, greeted by her friend of thirty years, the Grand Duchess Louise. For two weeks Clara was once again an intimate of the Badisch court. She and Louise renewed their friendship, spending much time together in the ducal apartments talking of many things, as two sisters might after they had been apart for some years. The parting words of the Duchess, Clara would always remember: "Tell them in America how much we love you. Tell them."[12]

This last trip to Europe turned into something of a grand tour—St. Petersburg, Moscow, Berlin, Karlsruhe, Paris. In the French capital she lingered for ten days, reliving the events of 1871 as she walked the streets, enjoying half-forgotten sights, Place Vendome with its great column once again in place, Les Invalides where Napoleon lay enshrined. She thought much about Napoleon when in Moscow and now again Paris. All that she had seen and done since coming to Europe, the great celebrations and visits to tombs of old personal friends in Switzerland had put Clara in a pensive mood. As the steamship *Pennsylvania* made its way westward Clara wondered about her life's work.

I fell into a revery myself as to how much reading I should have done, how much I should have lived with the literary world, if I had never heard of a Red Cross. Would it perhaps have been better if I never had, as it looks now. I almost *feel yes*. I cannot see that I have really established anything that is to *live*, or that is, *perhaps*, needed in a country like ours, and with a people so full of ready adaptation, and quick impulses . . . but if usefulness to the people, and my usefulness to it, have found an end, is to me the question of the moment—the *latter* seems to me very apparent, and the former is not for *me* to decide.[13]

Was Clara preparing herself mentally for giving up the fight, a fight she well knew awaited her sooner or later? Or had she found in Europe a depth of understanding and appreciation making her want to continue in the Red Cross presidency against all odds? She was bound to feel this tugging in opposed directions. And after all as she intimated it might not be her decision to make. People and events, considerations over which Clara was to have little control, were to provide a final answer.

Two formidable individuals were to run afoul Barton's ambitions for the Red Cross. One was Mabel Boardman, the other, Theodore Roosevelt. Both were powerful adversaries. Mabel Boardman had been one of the incorporators when the Red Cross was chartered by

Congress in 1900. She brought a rich and varied background to her interests and dedication to philanthropy. Of distinguished ancestry, her father was a wealthy Cleveland, Ohio, businessman who traced his roots back to William Bradford and Plymouth Plantation. He had married into an equally prominent family, the Sheffields of New Haven, best remembered for funding the Sheffield School of Science at Yale. Mabel Boardman, born in 1860, had a privileged upbringing with study at home and abroad and wide travel experience. She preferred Washington to Cleveland as a place to reside. Never to marry, she turned her considerable energy to a number of good causes: day nurseries, hospitals, and, at the time of the Spanish-American War, the recruitment of nurses. Considering herself a close student of the workings of the Red Cross in Europe Boardman became dissatisfied with the American association as Barton had developed it. At first neutral, she soon was in the forefront of the effort to bring about Clara's retirement. In the aftermath Boardman became the driving force as the American Red Cross was reorganized. She showed herself an able administrator that, combined with her wealth and social station, helped to account for both the defeat of Clara Barton and the successes of the Red Cross in the years thereafter.

If Mabel Boardman was the hammer that brought Barton to grief, Theodore Roosevelt was the anvil. Clara had had her brief but pleasant encounter with Colonel Roosevelt in Cuba in 1898. His impressions must have been positive because in his 1899 Annual Message as Governor of New York he proclaimed that the Red Cross had "done admirable work for our soldiers during the summer just past." And he added, "the Red Cross should be the right hand of the Medical Department of the army, in peace and war; for even the best medical department will always need volunteer aid in the case either of battles or of camp epidemics."[14] Clara had no occasion to have contact with Theodore Roosevelt again until the tragic death of McKinley. Because she had been successful in cultivating presidents over the years, Barton counted on good relations with the new administration, devastated though she was by the assassination of McKinley, her friend and patron. She forwarded copies of her annual Red Cross reports to

President Roosevelt in 1901 and 1902, and they were received without adverse comment. More significantly Barton and the president were the two leading guests of honor at the Spanish-American Veterans Convention in Detroit in the autumn of 1902. Theodore Roosevelt was the featured speaker and Clara made no move to upstage him, but did rival him in the applause they each received. By all accounts he was friendly and attentive to her. Barton was invited to sit on the president's right as the veterans marched past the reviewing stand. Given all this, Clara understandably believed that she was again to be on cordial terms with the president of the United States. It was all the more hurtful, therefore, when weeks later Roosevelt turned his back on her. Why he acted as he did is bound up in the details of the struggle between Barton and Boardman for control of the organization to which they were each devoted.

Clara was well aware that opposition to her leadership was solidifying and identified some members of the Board of Directors as the enemies who must be vanquished. If Boardman, Mussey, and company were ready to seek her ouster at the annual meeting in December of 1902, Barton anticipated their intention. Her plan to meet the threat was twofold. She was prepared to propose a new set of by-laws which, if adopted, would give her an iron grip by reason of the power to appoint all committee memberships. In addition, she wanted the Board of Directors to be abolished. This was a bold idea, a dangerous one, and it could not carry the day without some adroit maneuvering. Votes must be rounded up to support her proposals. The second part of her plan called for encouraging as many friendly members as possible to attend the December meeting. Those who could not attend were asked to give their proxies to Clara. She did not tell the faithful any more than she deemed they needed to know, describing her agenda for major reforms as "some slight changes."15 The outcome was exactly what she had hoped. Drastic alteration in the by-laws was approved, and Barton herself elected president of the American Red Cross for life. The tactics that had been used were easy to fault and many of her friends were put off by Barton's lack of candor. It is equally fair to argue that Clara acted as she had because she was in a fight for survival. Nor should she be criticized because she had outsmarted her opponents.

Clara was not to savor success except briefly. The opposition now firmly in the hands of Mabel Boardman decided to take the issues raised at the meeting directly to Theodore Roosevelt; as president he was, in keeping with precedent, the honorary chairman of the Red Cross Advisory Committee. In a letter to the president, Barton was charged by her enemies with an abuse of authority to the detriment of the Red Cross, portraying her as ready to ride roughshod over any who opposed her. Mention was made of "loose and improper arrangements in the accounting and the disbursement of the Society's funds."16 Boardman's social connections may have added to the credibility of this letter of indictment. She was a long-time friend of William Howard Taft, then serving as Roosevelt's secretary of war, and more significantly, Boardman was close to Anna Roosevelt Cowles, Theodore Roosevelt's sister. This consideration the president was not likely to allow to go unnoticed.

It was disingenuous on the part of Roosevelt, an inveterate writer of letters and someone who enjoyed verbal combat, to direct his secretary, George B. Cortelyou, to write to Barton in the matter. The implied accusation that Barton had engaged in a questionable use of funds was especially vindictive, yet the president seemed to take it at face value. She was guilty as charged. And worse was to follow. Under the new by-laws the president and his cabinet were constituted as a Board of Consultation of the Red Cross. Roosevelt dismissed this arrangement out of hand. The letter stated: "It is not possible for the President or any of his Cabinet to serve on such a Committee and the President directs me to request that you have it publicly announced that the President and his Cabinet cannot so serve."17 Down to this time, January, 1903, relations between Barton and Roosevelt would have to be described as cordial, and that makes his attitude and actions difficult to understand, much less to excuse. He had been kindly treated by her in their single encounter in Cuba. The Red Cross had reimbursed Roosevelt for the seven hundred fifty dollars he had paid at one time or another for Red Cross supplies, undoubtedly with

Clara's approval.[18] The highly visible cordiality in Detroit just a few months before turned suddenly to annoyance if not anger as Roosevelt cut the ground beneath her. Years later, in 1916, Roosevelt wrote to Mary Logan that he was "by no means favorably impressed by the type of work she [Barton] had done in the Spanish-American War."[19] By then Clara was dead and such a remark could be delivered with impunity. The question remains, why did he turn on Barton in 1903? Had Roosevelt expressed the view he shared with Logan in 1900 rather than sixteen years later, had he not honored Barton at the veterans convention, then his rejection of the Red Cross president might not have come as a surprise. Such circumstances would not, however, have justified his outright dismissal of Clara Barton, denying her the opportunity to tell her side of the story.

Once it was clear that the president would not grant her the interview she sought Barton had no choice but to respond to the Roosevelt and Cortelyou rejection notice by mail. She would write her own letter within the month. Her response has been variously characterized as "dignified" or "obsequious, almost whining."[20] Depending on which passages are cited it appears to have been both. Barton made no apology relative to the "charges" brought against her. In this respect she maintained a steady and unyielding stand, forthright in every way. But in making her case, she played up to the president, retreating to such phrases as "none better than your honored self . . . can better judge if the body of relief were aggressive in its conduct, imperious or unjust in its demands."[21] On the advice of friends Clara decided not to include some closing remarks which, as they are read today, show the extent to which she felt shamed by the president's treatment of her. She proposed to tell Roosevelt that he had given her no choice but to leave her country and settle permanently elsewhere. "My retirement will be absolute, out of the influence of all, and I will live out in another country the good faith I have always sought to cherish in my own." The letter as sent was signed "Your obedient countrywoman."[22] Would the receipt of the deleted words have made any difference of outcome? The question is moot, but the effects of presidential rejection reverberated for months to come. True-blue Mary Logan wrote to Cortelyou: "I do not think that he [Roosevelt] realizes that he has inflicted so serious a wound as he did by his letter."[23] The president was unmoved, except to endorse through another letter over Cortelyou's signature some vaguely worded notions about agreement between the factions as being "essential to good work."[24] It hardly amounted to a commitment, and he continued to ignore Barton's contention that she had been given no chance to defend herself before the president. It appears furthermore that the Roosevelt administration in general was hostile. In March, 1903, Secretary of State John Hay, quoting "Section 5 of the Act approved June 6, 1900 (Statutes-at-Large, volume 31, page 280) that the American National Red Cross shall give such information concerning its transactions and affairs as the Secretary of State may from time to time require" proceeded to ask Barton for a list of the names of the members of the society.[25] In response to Hay's pompously phrased request, Barton explained that she would comply as soon as the list came from the printer. She then lectured the secretary by reminding him that it did not take an act of Congress to bind the Red Cross to provide information. Such power arose from the treaty of acceptance by the Senate in 1882.[26] Within ten days Hay was back at her. "The list has not yet been received, and I beg to request your cooperation in having it sent without delay" he wrote sharply.[27] Hay was surely making mountains out of molehills. But why?

Later, but before Clara announced her resignation as Red Cross president, Secretary of War Taft, writing in the *Army-Navy Register*, delivered a stinging rebuke:

The present state of the Red Cross [is] deplorable. It cannot be conducted by the people who have hitherto had charge of its affairs and retain public confidence and encouragement.[28]

Was Taft speaking for the president as well as for himself?

The private squabble soon became public property. The "remonstrants" as the Boardman-led contingent was called, sent a petition to Congress, the purpose being to alert that body to the need for a drastic overhaul of the Red Cross, one that would exclude Clara

Barton except possibly as an annuitant, honorary president. Barton had only dwindling forces to rally to her side as more and more members of the organization broke ranks and lined up with the remonstrants. In this situation Clara continued to believe that her long-standing reputation as an American heroine would be sufficient to protect her from ultimate defeat. Practical measures were in order nonetheless. She proceeded to dismiss from the executive committee Mabel Boardman, Anna Roosevelt Cowles, and all other members who had signed the letter sent to the president in December. The remonstrants, protesting that the by-laws under which this dismissal had been ordered were themselves illegal, ignored Barton's banishment of them. Vowing that they did not intend any personal attack on Barton, Boardman and company were then invited to rejoin the executive committee. What this accomplished was to bring the issue back to square one: Was the Red Cross to stay in the hands of Clara Barton, who was thought to have her face to the past, or was the Red Cross to free itself from Barton's control and enter a new phase of growth and prosperity under new leadership? To put this question a different way: Would Barton yield her presidency gracefully or must she be forced from office?[29]

In her own words, 1903 was "a hard and terrible year" for Barton when "all the scuril of the press has been poured over me like the filth of a sewer."[30] There were but few uplifting moments. One, a call from the people of Butler, Pennsylvania, in early December energized her, however briefly. The town was suffering from an epidemic of typhoid fever, and a number of the population had died. The weather was foul at that time of year, and Butler was three hundred miles from Glen Echo but Barton was determined to go. It proved to be a flying trip with a stay of only forty-eight hours. She distributed some supplies and provided money to purchase more. Again, as it had been at Galveston, it was her presence that gave heart to the stricken people of the town. There was still magic left in the Barton name and the Barton way of doing things in the field.

The annual December meeting of the Red Cross took place soon after Clara was back in Washington. Happily for her it lacked the rancor of the gathering of the year before. Boardman and her followers absented themselves, and with attendees generally favorable to her, Barton was confirmed as lifetime president and new by-laws were approved. The consensus of those present was that for its own good name a report of the association's activities and finances, going back to the year of the Johnstown flood, ought to be undertaken. Clara agreed to provide all the evidence in her possession and indeed was eager to do so. Only in this way could the proper image of the Red Cross be preserved. A committee was named to conduct the inquiry with Senator Proctor as its chairman. It was March before the first hearing was held.

Was Clara Barton on trial? She perceived the committee's purpose would be akin to have her standing at the bar all the while retaining her belief in the fair-mindedness of Senator Proctor. Charges in the strict sense had not been filed against her but there were some parts of the Barton record inviting scrutiny. The assumption of maladministration and questionable financial practices were two such concerns; these had been bruited about in the press and among those who had taken sides in the ongoing debate about Barton's conduct of Red Cross business. Clara plainly had her defenders, including Walter Phillips, the old newspaper friend who had been in the fight to bring the Red Cross to America. He published a pamphlet, *Some Facts Concerning Clara Barton's Work*, that challenged her defamers on all counts. Susan B. Anthony came to her defense calling the whole matter a "mean and despicable business."[31] Tillinghurst of Iowa stood firmly by her side and of course the Sheldons, Mary Logan, and Julian Hubbell. The prospect of the hearing remained daunting. Clara knew there were many loose ends in her conduct of Red Cross operations, the result of administrative style and not due to any intent to confuse or defraud. In the hands of enemies such things could be exaggerated or even distorted possibly to the level of charging malfeasance in office. Investigations have a way of veering in unexpected directions. The complaints as stated were virtually open-ended. They included the failure on Barton's part to develop the American Red Cross in the same way as had occurred in several European countries, violation of the by-laws, especially in the use of proxy votes, the use of relief funds raised for one project but spent in part at least on another, and finally the failure to keep complete records of funds received and disbursed. To defend her against these and other charges that might arise, Clara retained two lawyers, L. A. Stebbins and Thomas S. Hopkins.

Neither Barton nor her supporters were prepared for the testimony of John Morlan, the man who had betrayed her trust in managing Red Cross Park. He had written Anna Roosevelt Cowles claiming to have evidence to confirm Barton's questionable conduct of Red Cross money matters.[32] Furthermore Morlan was in frequent communication with Mabel Boardmen on the matter, and it is at least possible that he was in her pay.[33] Morlan testified that Red Cross money had been used to close the deal on the Park, that money raised for Russian relief had found its way to Texas. He told the committee that he was prepared to provide documentary evidence of his assertions upon his return the next day. When he failed to appear and his whereabouts were unknown, it became clear to all but the most prejudiced that Morlan's testimony was worthless. Because he was the only witness to appear before the committee, Barton's vindication appeared all the more likely. Henry Potter, the Episcopal bishop of New York, and Spencer Trask who had had a falling-out with Barton over Armenian relief weighed in against her, but with the vaguest assertions of wrongdoing. By that time Proctor had had enough. He abruptly declared the hearing over, characterizing it as the "most outrageous proceeding that has ever come under my observation."[34] Clara was relieved and pleased that the senator had acted so decisively but admitted that the outcome would be looked upon in some quarters as inconclusive, that her reputation was still under a cloud. She thought of herself as "hanging between heaven and earth."[35] On May 14, less than a fortnight after the committee had been dismissed, Clara Barton resigned her lifelong presidency of the American Red Cross. She severed all connection with the organization she had founded, nurtured, had lived for, and would have died for. She made this total break with what for thirty years had been the nerve center of her existence because she had been rejected. She could read the events of the previous months, and in years to come, in no other way, and they hardly may be interpreted otherwise.

Surveying the road she had traveled since serving with the Rough Riders in Cuba in 1898 the deciding turn occurred in January, 1903, when Barton received the letter from *the* Rough Rider himself. By her own estimate she had had dealings with every president from Lincoln to McKinley prior to her fateful encounter with Roosevelt. It made for a strange and unpredictable ending to a great career and cast a shadow over the years left to her. As for Roosevelt's reasons, the source of his disdain for Clara Barton, that remains puzzling. Had his judgment been warped as a result of conversations, unrecorded, with his sister Anna, or had Taft, because of his friendship with Boardman spoken out against Barton? Had some other member of the Ohio Gang, for example, Mark Hanna who like Boardman was from Cleveland and a combination of businessman and politician defamed her, with or without Boardman's encouragement? John Hay, another Ohioan, given his arched letters to Barton, is also suspect. Should speculation delve even more deeply into the motives behind Roosevelt's behavior? Did he resent the fact that he had turned to a little old lady to get much prized supplies while in Cuba, and for that reason had not made mention of the incident with only a passing reference to Barton and the Red Cross in his colorful account of the Rough Riders? What of the further fact that Miss Barton, when in her forties, had served heroically in the Civil War but Roosevelt's father avoided army service, however valid his reasons for doing so? That was always a touchy matter with the warrior side of Roosevelt's personality. Whatever the case, the president's treatment of Clara Barton was out of character for a man who was immensely respectful of womanhood and ever the public advocate of fair play.

## NOTES

1. Alfred D. Chandler, *The Managerial Revolution in American Business*, Cambridge: Harvard University Press, 1977, p. 6.

2. Barton to Joseph Gardner, July 10, 1899, Clara Barton *Papers*, Library of Congress.

3. Elizabeth B. Pryor, *Clara Barton: Professional Angel*, Philadelphia: University of Pennsylvania Press, 1981, p. 332.

4. Foster R. Dulles, *The American Red Cross: A History*, New York: Harper and Brothers, 1950, pp. 63–65.

5. Pryor, *Professional Angel*, p. 327.

6. Clara Barton, *Story of the Red Cross*, New York: Airmont Publishing Company, 1968, pp. 108–109.

7. Barton Journal, Dec. 12, 1900, Clara Barton *Papers*.

8. Pryor, *Professional Angel*, p. 329.

9. Ishbel Ross, *Clara Barton: Angel of the Battlefield*, Indianapolis: Bobbs Merrill, 1949, p. 233.

10. Blanche C. Williams, *Clara Barton: Daughter of Destiny*, Philadelphia: J. P. Lippincott Company, 1941, p. 309.

11. Ross, *Angel of the Battlefield*, p. 233.

12. Pryor, *Professional Angel*, p. 337.

13. Ross, *Angel of the Battlefield*, p. 237.

14. Roosevelt, "Annual Message" New York Governor, January, 1899, *The Works of Theodore Roosevelt*, 24 volumes, New York: Charles Scribner Sons, 1924, vol. 17, p. 19.

15. Pryor, *Professional Angel*, p. 338.

16. Foster R. Dulles, *The American Red Cross: A History*, New York: Harper and Brothers, 1950, p. 71.

17. George B. Cortelyou to Clara Barton, January 2, 1903, American National Red Cross *Papers*, Library of Congress.

18. Sylvia Jukes Morris, *Edith Kermit Roosevelt: Portrait of a First Lady*, New York: Coward, McCann & Geoghegan, Inc., 1980, p. 186.

19. Roosevelt to Mary Logan, June 26, 1916, Theodore Roosevelt *Papers*, Library of Congress.

20. Ross, *Angel of the Battlefield*, p. 245; Pryor, *Professional Angel*, p. 339.

21. Ross, *Angel of the Battlefield*, p. 245.

22. Ibid., Appendix 10, p. 285.

23. Ibid., p. 245.

24. Ibid.

25. Williams, *Daughter of Destiny*, Appendix C, p. 448.

26. Ibid., pp. 448–49.

27. Ibid., p. 449.

28. Clyde E. Buckingham, *Clara Barton, A Broad Humanity*, Alexandria, Va.: Privately published, 1980, p. 307

29. Dulles, *The American Red Cross*, pp. 72–73.

30. Williams, *Daughter of Destiny*, p. 409.

31. Ross, *Angel of the Battlefield*, p. 247.

32. Anna Roosevelt Cowles to Theodore Roosevelt, Feb. 21, 1903, Theodore Roosevelt *Papers*.

33. Buckingham, *Clara Barton, A Broad Humanity*, p. 309, p. 313, f.n. 21; 22.

34. Pryor, *Professional Angel*, p. 353.

35. Ibid.

# — 7 —

# *Last Years, Last Words*

The last years of Clara Barton were ones of sadness and disappointment, of that there can be no doubt and no surprise. She kept busy
with things that mattered a little, or mattered not at all. A life that for
so many years was sharply focused now appeared directionless. Barton
treasured her reputation as she reflected on her life and work. *The
Story of My Childhood*, published in 1907, was projected as the first in
a series of short books which, when completed, would constitute an
autobiography. Beyond 1907 nothing was forthcoming, however. Was
Clara too old to sum up all that she had done and tried to do, too
tired, too defeated? Very probably all these considerations combined
to explain why someone as prolific as Barton was in correspondence
and in her diary, and as satisfying as it would have been for her to tell
her story, failed to leave a written testament of achievement. Clara had
entered the final phase of her life. Because she realized this she had
recourse to mediums, doubtless to seek assurance where she could find
it, that her years had been well and wisely spent.

Barton's last words, therefore, tended to center on death as on the
meaning of her life. She wrote to the Grand Duchess Louise: "They
tell me I am changing worlds, and one of my last thoughts and wishes
is to tell you of my unchanging love and devotion to you."[1] Coming
just two months to the day before her death it was intended as a fond
farewell. Earlier in her life the specter of suicide stalked her, only to

be pushed aside by renewed commitment and renewed activity. When nature imposed its will and the moment had come for her to leave the world, to pass over, she spoke directly to the issue. Clara's final words: "Let me go, let me go,"[2] whispered to Julian Hubbell and Stevé who were at her bedside, strongly suggest that she was prepared to enter the spirit world where she might expect to commune with family and old friends. As for words after death Barton left a request that at her funeral among the hymns to be sung was "Jesus, Lover Of My Soul." Her faith was indeed an odd mixture, but vital and purposeful nonetheless.[3]

In 1904 death was years away. To detach herself from worries, and they were not insignificant ones, she turned to the National First Aid Association. It proved a salutary outlet. "The First Aid is all that in *any* way reconciles me to the fact that I did not leave the country on the receipt of President Roosevelt's letter. The impulse to do so was almost stronger than the ties of life."[4] The severe wounds thus began to heal. Even so worries persisted. They were inspired largely by the administration that had taken over the Red Cross in Washington. The new president was former Admiral William Van Reypen with Mabel Boardman lurking immediately in the background. At the time Boardman was of a mind that only a man should be the formal head of the society. At first Van Reypen proposed to press the inquiry regarding Barton's use of Red Cross funds. Then he demanded that she, having title to certain Red Cross property, must turn it over to the society, even though Barton had helped to purchase it with her own money. Barton acquiesced in order to avoid court action. At one juncture Clara feared the house at Glen Echo would be denied her. In the midst of such worries Clara Barton, the great Civil War heroine, thought seriously of leaving her native land to settle in Mexico, perhaps, where she might take the lead in establishing a Mexican Red Cross. Friends and the unshakable good will of the Grand Army of the Republic (GAR) persuaded her to give up so drastic a move.[5]

One such friend was Edward Howe. He had encouraged Barton to use the Red Cross to promote a subsidiary society, a First Aid Association. That was in 1902.[6] Basic to his plan was a set of instructions to teach the average citizen how to administer first aid to the sick and injured. Barton was instantly enthusiastic, arguing that much of what she had done in wartime was nothing more or less than first aid, extending life for some and making less painful the death of others. The idea did not catch on, in spite of Clara's endorsement. Now, three years later, Howe had established a National First Aid Association and invited Barton to join him in promoting it. She lent her name to the group, spoke on various occasions to encourage people to see the value of emergency first aid, and gave small sums of money as needed. These activities helped fill the void that had become her life and at the same time were appropriate to her diminished energies.

Barton tried to pay as little attention as possible to the Red Cross which faced its first great post-Barton crisis with the San Francisco earthquake of 1906. It was a major catastrophe and President Roosevelt, perhaps eager to justify the wisdom of the change in command that he had brought about, called upon the society to meet the challenge. Indeed, he announced that the Red Cross was the organization best prepared to handle this multidimensional tragedy. It was, of course, ill prepared to do so. Before long Roosevelt had to withdraw from the Red Cross the responsibility of distributing public funds for San Francisco, concluding that he had given it too much power.[7] Clara Barton perhaps may be forgiven her small squeal of delight when the Red Cross showed itself unable to measure up to the president's expectations. Had Roosevelt obtained a fuller awareness of the strengths and limitations of the society, whether under the leadership of Barton or Van Reypen, he would not have acted so impulsively. One has only to recall Barton's extreme caution in committing the Red Cross to the overall management of disaster recovery to justify criticism of Roosevelt's ignorance of the nature and reality of relief work, and therefore his precipitous action.

In spite of depression and physical infirmities Barton refused to become a recluse. She was in demand as a speaker, or more usually as a presence at various gatherings, including the encampments of the GAR. In 1905 she went to Boston to attend a meeting of the New England Woman Suffrage Association, sharing the platform with

Susan B. Anthony and Julia Ward Howe. The next year she was in Baltimore where she spoke to other suffragists and was honored at dinner. As late as 1910 Barton, unaccompanied, made the trip to Chicago, and in the meantime had traveled each year to North Oxford where she had bought a summer home. She was often the subject of interviews, on one occasion by Ida M. Tarbell who was doing a series of articles for *American Magazine* telling the stories of the nation's most famous women.[8] While living at Glen Echo Clara kept her own house, did the chores, maintained the place in good order inside and out, trimming the hedges and shoveling snow. Almost to the last, activity was the watchword for her.

Not even such distractions could offset a growing preoccupation with death, a state of mind fed by the passing of friends: Susan B. Anthony, Julia Ward Howe, Dorence Atwater, Henri Dunant, Abby Sheldon, and Mary Baker Eddy among them. As she grappled with the fact of death for others and the prospect of it for herself she appears to have put great faith in mediums. She attended weekly séances conducted by Mrs. Warneke in her parlor in Washington. According to Barton's diary entries she had been spoken to by Lincoln and Grant, by her sister, Dolly, and by Theodore Parker. One account described how General Grant assured her that Theodore Roosevelt "had made a mess of the Red Cross," adding he "is so bull-headed he will never retract anything; in fact, he really makes himself believe he is right."[9] Clearly Roosevelt's 1903 letter and his subsequent treatment of Barton continued to invade her thoughts or dreams. Clara persisted in taking her sessions with Warneke seriously even after the Grand Duchess Louise reacted coldly to her accounts of contacts with the dead.

Simultaneously Barton felt a strong attraction to the teachings of Christian Science as expounded by Mary Baker Eddy in her book *Science and Health*. If Christian Science taught no more than a sophisticated understanding of mind over matter Clara had no difficulty identifying with it. On a number of occasions she had been ailing physically to the point of incapacitation, only to rise from her sickbed and by sheer will power carry on her work. She termed Mrs. Eddy "the greatest living American woman" but never joined the Church of Christ, Scientist.[10] By temperament Clara was not a joiner, at least not of the churches, never having formally become a member of the family's Universalist congregation in North Oxford. Her religious sense was highly personalized, though it derived from the New Testament. "In as much as ye have done it unto the least of my brethren, ye have done it unto Me," was the scriptural text that guided her actions according to the best testimony.[11] To Judge A. W. Terrell in April, 1911, she wrote: "I was born to liberal views and have lived a liberal creed." Having affirmed a belief in the divinity of Christ she went on to explain that "it would be difficult for me to stop there and believe that this spark of divinity was accorded to no other of God's creation."[12] Such a passage is redolent of Emersonian idealism that Clara could have readily encountered had she not discovered it herself. For her, Christianity was not a profession of beliefs but action taken toward all mankind based on those beliefs. She felt no need for apology or explanation. In her own words: "I have lived much that I have not written, but I have written nothing I have not lived."[13]

Upon her death the tributes, especially in the newspapers, were glowing. Beyond that, many of the comments were astute. The *New York Globe*: "Her religion ran to the whole of mankind. . . . She not only preached but practiced the new internationalism. . . . Give the world enough Clara Bartons and the brotherhood of man will be ushered in." This message was echoed by the *Richmond Journal*. "Clara Barton was a woman of large vision and great heart. She answered the call for service in its broadest sense." Two papers, the *New York Post* and the *Boston Transcript*, drew a parallel between Florence Nightingale and Clara. Read the *Post* editorial: "The nineteenth century produced no finer figures than Florence Nightingale and Clara Barton." It remained for the Rockford (Illinois) *Register* to note that no representative of President Taft or the American National Red Cross was in attendance at her funeral. Clara probably would have preferred it that way.[14]

The comparison between Barton and Nightingale is historically appropriate. Plutarch himself, had he sought for lives of eminent contemporary Britons and Americans, could have done no better than to proclaim these two Victorian women.[15] They came of age about the same time and accomplished great things through their humanitarian endeavors. Nightingale's ministrations to sick and wounded British soldiers during the Crimean War became legendary even in America. Within years Barton would be emulating her feats of compassion during the Civil War. Barton and Nightingale were both realists. They did not seek an end to wars; their calling was to ameliorate war's frightening effects. The gossamer of popular memory of them as unspoiled heroines is quickly blown away by the winds of truth, revealing in each of them a greatness discoverable through sober contemplation of their work. What they accomplished was real. In her later endeavors the level of public health became a matter of national concern for Nightingale as she battled stand-pat politicians unwilling to accept reforms. As for Barton her contribution to the Geneva Convention of the American Amendment spoke the urgent need to provide assistance in the wake of manmade and natural disasters. Barton's founding of the American Red Cross, as she struggled against official indifference, was part of the self-help spirit that had characterized America. In her life of service Clara Barton was being true to her country and true to herself.

## NOTES

1. Barton to Grand Duchess Louise, Feb. 12, 1912, Ishbel Ross, *Clara Barton: Angel of the Battlefield*, Indianapolis: Bobbs Merrill, 1949, p. 267.

2. Blanche C. Williams, *Clara Barton: Daughter of Destiny*, Philadelphia: J. P. Lippincott Company, 1941, p. 435.

3. William E. Barton, *The Life of Clara Barton*, 2 vols., New York: AMS Press, 1969, vol. 2, p. 317.

4. Ross, *Angel of the Battlefield*, p. 258.

5. Elizabeth B. Pryor, *Clara Barton: Professional Angel*, Philadelphia: University of Pennsylvania Press, 1981, p. 357.

6. Ibid., p. 358.

7. Elizabeth Brown Pryor, *Clara Barton*, Washington, D.C.: National Park Service, 1981, p. 59.

8. Ross, *Angel of the Battlefield*, Appendix 11, p. 285.

9. Williams, *Daughter of Destiny*, p. 429.

10. William E. Barton, *The Life of Clara Barton*, vol. 2, p. 318.

11. Percy Epler, *The Life of Clara Barton*, New York: Macmillan, 1915, p. 410.

12. Ibid., pp. 410–411.

13. Clara Barton, *A Story of the Red Cross*, New York: Airmont Publishing Company, 1968, p. 9.

14. Ross, *Angel of the Battlefield*, Appendix 13, pp. 288–289.

15. David H. Burton, *An Anglo-American Plutarch*, Lanham, Md.: University Press of America, 1990, pp. 105–128.

# Bibliography

## PRIMARY SOURCES–UNPUBLISHED

Clara Barton *Papers*–Library of Congress.
National Red Cross *Papers*–Library of Congress.
Theodore Roosevelt *Papers*–Library of Congress.

## PRIMARY SOURCES–PUBLISHED

Barton, Clara, *The Red Cross of the Geneva Convention: What It Is*, Washington, D.C.: Privately printed, 1872.

Barton, Clara, *The Red Cross in Peace and War*, Washington, D.C.: Historical Press, 1899.

Barton, Clara, *The Red Cross: A History of This Remarkable Movement*, Washington, D.C.: Privately printed, 1872.

Barton, Clara, *The Story of My Childhood*, Meriden, Conn.: Journal Publishing Company, 1907.

Barton, Clara, *A Story of the Red Cross*, New York: Airmont Publishing Company, 1968.

## SECONDARY SOURCES–BIOGRAPHICAL

Barton, William E., *The Life of Clara Barton*, 2 vols., New York: AMS Press, 1969.

Buckingham, Clyde E., *Clara Barton, A Broad Humanity*, Alexandria, Va.: Privately published, 1980.

Epler, Percy, *The Life of Clara Barton*, New York: Macmillan, 1915.

Oates, Stephen B., *A Woman of Valor, Clara Barton and the Civil War*, New York: The Free Press, 1994.

Pryor, Elizabeth B., *Clara Barton*, Washington, D.C.: National Park Service, 1981.

Pryor, Elizabeth B., *Clara Barton: Professional Angel*, Philadelphia: University of Pennsylvania Press, 1988.

Ross, Ishbel, *Clara Barton: Angel of the Battlefield*, Indianapolis: Bobbs Merrill, 1949.

Williams, Blanche C., *Clara Barton: Daughter of Destiny*, Philadelphia: J. P. Lippincott Company, 1941.

## SECONDARY SOURCES–SPECIAL

### Books

Burton, David H., *An Anglo-American Plutarch*, Lanham, Md.: University Press of America, 1990.

Conklin, William, ed., *Clara Barton and Dansville*, Dansville: N.Y.P.A. Owen Publishing Company, 1966.

Young, Charles S., *Clara Barton: A Centenary Tribute*, Boston: Gorham Press, 1922.

### Articles

Harris, Joel Chandler, "The Sea Island Hurricane: The Relief of the Sea Islands," *Scribner's Magazine*, v. 15, n. 3, March, 1894, pp. 265–275.

Welter, Barbara, "The Cult of True Womanhood, 1820–1860," *American Quarterly*, 18 (1966), pp. 151–174.

Williams, Sophie, "Miss Barton and the Red Cross," *The Review of Reviews*, v. 9, n. 50, March, 1894, pp. 310–323.

## SECONDARY SOURCES–GENERAL

Adams, George, *Doctors in Blue*, New York: Henry Schuman, 1952.

Barton, George, *Angels of the Battlefield*, Philadelphia: The Catholic Art Publishing Co., 1898.

Basler, Roy P., *Abraham Lincoln: His Speeches and Writings*, Cleveland and New York: World Publishing Company, 1946.

Binder, Frederick, *The Age of the Common School, 1830–1845*, New York: John Wiley, 1974.

Brockett, L. P., *Women's Work in the Civil War*, Philadelphia: Zeigler, McCurdy and Co., 1967.

Cassara, Ernest, ed., *Universalism in America*, Boston: Beacon Press, 1971.

Chandler, Alfred D., *The Managerial Revolution in American Business*, Cambridge: Harvard University Press, 1977.

Curti, Merle, *American Philanthropy Abroad*, New Brunswick: Rutgers University Press, 1963.

Dulles, Foster R., *The American Red Cross: A History*, New York: Harper and Brothers, 1950.

Dulles, Foster R., *Prelude To World Power*, New York: Macmillan, 1965.

Flexner, Eleanor, *A Century of Struggle*, New York: Atheneum, 1974.

Futch, Ovid, *A History of Andersonville Prison*, Gainesville: University of Florida Press, 1968.

Gordon, Michael, *The American Family in Socio-Historical Perspective*, New York: St. Martin's Press, 1978.

Kernoble, Portia, *The Red Cross Nurse in Action, 1882–1948*, New York: Harper Brothers, 1949.

Leech, Margaret, *Reveille in Washington*, New York: Harper Brothers, 1941.

Leiby, James, *A History of Social Welfare and Social Work in the United States*, New York: Columbia University Press, 1978.

Maxwell, William Q., *Lincoln's Fifth Wheel*, New York: Longsman Green, 1956.

McCullough, David, *The Johnstown Flood*, New York: Simon and Schuster, 1968.

McPherson, James M., *Battle Cry of Freedom*, New York: Oxford University Press, 1988

Nye, Gerald P., *The Cultural Life of the New Nation*, New York: Harper Brothers, 1960.

Plesur, Milton, *America's Outward Thrust Approaches in Foreign Affairs, 1865–1890*, DeKalb: Northern Illinois University Press, 1971.

Roosevelt, Theodore, *The Works of Theodore Roosevelt*, 24 vols. Memorial Edition, New York: Charles Scribner's Sons, 1924.

Wishy, Bernard, *The Child and the Republic*, Philadelphia: University of Pennsylvania Press, 1968.

# Index

American Amendment (to the Geneva Convention for the Amelioration of the Condition of the Wounded and Sick Armies in the Field), 110–11, 115, 122, 164

American Red Cross: in Armenia, 128–30; in Cuba, 132–36, 139, 141–43; disaster relief work before 1885, 100–101, 105, 107–9; disaster relief work from 1885 to 1906, 113, 116–21, 125–27, 143–45, 161; federal charter, 122, 142–43, 145, 152; founding, 84–94; local chapters, 94, 99, 100–101, 118, 141–42; the managerial revolution and, 139–41, 143, 145; relationship with international movement, 85, 93, 95, 105, 110, 132–33; in Russia, 122–23. *See also* American Amendment; Barton, Clara

Andersonville, Ga., Prison, 54–56
Andrew, Gov. John A., 32
Annapolis, Md., 51–53
Anthony, Susan B., 154, 162
Antietam, battle of, 39–40
Antislavery, 4, 21
Appia, Dr. Louis, 66, 68, 85, 89, 94, 107, 110
Armenians, Turkish massacre and persecution of, 128–30
Arthur, Chester A., 93, 95
Atwater, Dorence, 54–55, 57, 58–59, 75, 76, 162
Augusta, Empress of Germany, 111, 112

Baltzley, Edward, 140
Baltzley, Edwin, 140
Barker, Abby, 14
Barker, Louise, 13–14
Barton, Clara: as administrator of the American Red Cross, 100, 105, 112–13, 116, 118, 128, 140; as "Angel of the Battle-

field," 37–38, 43, 59, 61; as architect of the American Red Cross, 99, 107–9, 111, 113, 115; Armenian relief efforts, 128–30, 155; celebrity status, 59, 112, 116, 146; childhood and adolescence, 3–9; during the Civil War and its aftermath, 27–61 (*see also names of specific battles*); compared with Florence Nightingale, 59, 68, 77–78, 163–64; controversy over leadership approach of, 127, 145, 149–55; Cuban relief efforts, 132–34, 142; education, 7, 13–14; as founder of the American Red Cross, 84–95, 164; during the Franco-Prussian War and its aftermath, 70–76; "Have Ye Room?", 79; as head of Sherborn (Mass.) Reformatory Prison for Women, 102–5; last years, 159–63; lecturing career, 57–59; mental health of, 23, 47, 70, 77, 81–82, 141–42; as patent office clerk, 19–22, 27–28, 31, 47; physical health of, 40, 67, 78, 81–82, 162; *The Red Cross of the Geneva Convention: What It Is*, 86–87; sensitivity to criticism, 50, 82, 151, 160, 162; during the Spanish-American War, 134–36, 139, 141, 150–51, 156; *The Story of My Childhood*, 159; teaching career, 9–12, 15–18

Barton, David (Clara's brother), 6–8, 13, 23, 43–44, 46
Barton, Dorothea "Dolly" (Clara's sister), 5, 162
Barton, Sarah Stone (Clara's mother), 3, 4–5, 8, 14, 21, 60
Barton, Sarah "Sally" (Clara's sister) (Mrs. Vester Vassall), 6, 22–23, 40, 53, 67, 78, 82
Barton, Capt. Stephen (Clara's father), 3–4, 12, 23, 26, 31–32
Barton, Stephen (Clara's brother), 5–6, 12, 13, 14, 18, 50–51
Barton, Stephen E. (Stevé)(Clara's nephew), 91, 132, 142, 160
Barton, William, 82, 91
Belo, Colonel, 114–15
Bismarck, Count Otto von, 70, 74, 76
Blaine, James G., 91–93, 95
Blue Anchor, 94, 99–100
Boardman, Mabel, 147–48, 150, 153, 154, 155, 156, 160
Bordentown, N.J., 16–17, 30
Bowles, Charles S. F., 68
Brown, Rev. John, 114
Bull Run, battles of, 31, 35–38
Bunnell, Mark, 101
Butler, Benjamin F., 49, 50, 51, 90, 102–3, 105
Butler, Pa., typhoid fever epidemic of 1903 in, 153

Cedar Mountain, battle of, 34–35
Cedarville, N.J., 15, 17
Central Cuban Relief Committee, 132, 134, 135
Chaddock, Mahala, 107

Charleston, S.C., earthquake of
    1886 in, 115–16
Childs, Fanny, 18
Cleveland, Grover, 114–15
Clinton Liberal Institute, 18–19
Cold Harbor, battle of, 49
Conger, Sen. Omar D., 92
Cotton Centennial Exposition,
    112
Cowles, Anna Roosevelt, 150,
    153, 155, 156
Cuba, plight of reconcentrados in,
    131–33

Dansville, N.Y., 82, 83, 89, 94,
    106, 107, 112
DeFreize, John D., 84
DeWitt, Rep. Alexander, 19, 22
Dix, Dorothea, 27, 43, 47, 80, 94
Dunant, Jean Henri, 66, 68, 87,
    111, 162
Dunn, Dr. James, 37, 39–40

Eddy, Mary Baker, 162
Elwell, Col. John, 44–45
Ely, Joshua, 16
Evarts, William, 88, 91

Fifteenth Amendment, 60
Fifty-fourth Regiment (Mass.),
    45, 60
First Aid, 160–61
Fowler, L. N., 8, 23, 77
Fredericksburg, battle of, 41–42
Frelinghuysen, Frederick T., 95,
    110

Gage, Frances, 45, 46, 47, 57–58,
    94
Galveston, Tex., hurricane and
    tidal wave of 1900 in, 143–
    45
Gardner, Dr. Joseph, 123–24,
    135, 136
Garfield, James A., 90–93
Geneva Convention for the Ame-
    lioration of the Condition of
    the Wounded and Sick Armies
    in the Field, 66–67, 68, 92–
    93, 95, 129, 132. *See also*
    American Amendment
Gillmore, Gen. Quincy, 44, 45–
    46
Glen Echo, Md., 140–41, 160,
    162
Golay, Jules, 53, 67–68
Grand Army of the Republic
    (GAR), 89–90, 94, 160, 161
Greeley, Horace, 57

Hale, Robert, 87–88
Harris, Joel Chandler, 126–27
"Have Ye Room?" (Barton), 79
Hay, John, 152, 156
Hayes, Lucy, 88
Hayes, Rutherford B., 88, 89
Hightstown, N.J., 15–16, 30
Hilton Head, S.C., 43–47
Holmes, Mr. and Mrs. Joseph,
    77
Hopkins, Thomas S., 155
Howe, Edward, 160
Howe, Julia Ward, 78, 162
Hubbell, Dr. Julian: as aide to
    Clara Barton, 106, 112, 114,

154, 160; American disaster relief work, 94, 101, 107, 116–17; international disaster relief work, 123, 129, 135, 142

International Red Cross movement. *See* Red Cross

Jackson, Dr. James, 82–83
Jacksonville, Fla., yellow fever epidemic of 1888 in, 117–18
Johnstown, Pa., flood of 1889 in, 119–21

Kennan, George, 90
Klopisch, Louis, 132, 134

Lawrence, Judge William, 93, 100
Lee, Enola, 107, 117
Lincoln, Robert Todd, 92
Logan, Gen. John A., 90, 94
Logan, Mary (Mrs. John A.), 146, 151–52, 154
Louise, Grand Duchess of Baden: during the Franco-Prussian War and its aftermath, 72–74, 76; friendship with Clara Barton, 84, 85, 111, 146–47, 159, 162

Margot, Antoinette, 71, 73, 76
Mason, Charles, 19–21, 22
McClelland, Robert, 20
McKinley, William, 132–34, 141–43, 148

Mississippi River, flooding of, 101, 105–6, 108
Moore, Capt. James, 55, 57
Morlan, John, 117, 124, 155
Mount Vernon, Ill., tornado of 1888 in, 116–17
Moynier, Gustave: as advisor and friend of Clara Barton, 71, 85–86, 94, 95, 110; role in Red Cross movement, 66, 68, 92–93
Mussey, Ellen Spencer, 144, 146, 149

National First Aid Association, 160–61
North Oxford, Mass., 3, 11–12, 20, 29–30, 162
Norton, Charles, 15, 16
Norton, Mary, 14, 15, 16, 44

Office of Correspondence with Friends of the Missing Men of the United States Army, 51–54, 56–60
Ohio River, flooding of, 101, 105–7

Phillips, Walter, 90, 154
Phrenology, 8
Poor, Mattie, 23
Potter, Henry (bishop of N.Y.), 155
Proctor, Sen. Redfield, 133–34, 154, 155

Ramsay, Samuel, 14, 20, 53

Red Cross (international movement): during the Franco-Prussian War, 71–73, 75; history, 66–67; relationship with the American Red Cross, 85, 93, 95, 105, 110, 116, 132–33. *See also* American Amendment; American Red Cross; Geneva Convention for the Amelioration of the Condition of the Wounded and Sick Armies in the Field

*The Red Cross of the Geneva Convention: What It Is* (Barton), 86–87

Red Cross Park (Bedford, Ind.), 123–24, 155

Roosevelt, Theodore, 136, 147–52, 156, 161, 162

Rucker, Col. Daniel, 33–34, 39

Russia, famine of 1890s in, 122–23

San Francisco, earthquake of 1906 in, 161

Schieren, Charles, 132

Sea Islands of South Carolina, hurricane of 1893 in, 124–27

Seward, Frederick, 88

Seward, William, 68, 87, 88, 91

Sheldon, Abby, 77, 154, 162

Sheldon, Joseph, 57, 77, 94, 110, 154

Sherborn (Mass.) Reformatory Prison for Women, 102–5

Simpson, Adm. Willis T., 134, 135

Solomons, Adolphus, 109, 110

*Some Facts Concerning Clara Barton's Work* (Phillips), 154

Southmayd, Col. R. C., 117–18

Spiritualism, 159, 162

Spotsylvania Court House, battle of, 48–49

Stebbins, L. A., 155

Sternberg, Surgeon Gen. George M., 135

Stone, Elvira, 28, 30, 83

*The Story of My Childhood* (Barton), 159

Taft, William Howard, 150, 152, 156, 163

Tarbell, Ida M., 162

Terrell, Judge A. W., 163

Texas, drought of 1885–86 in, 114

Tillinghurst, Benjamin F., 123, 154

Tillman, Gov. Benjamin, 125

Tolstoi, Count Leo, 123

Trask, Spencer, 129, 155

Universal Peace Union, 111

Universalism, 3, 13, 163

Upton, Mr. and Mrs. C. H., 68, 69

Van Reypen, Adm. William, 160, 161

Vassall, Irving, 22–23, 51

Vassall, Mrs. Vester. *See* Barton, Sarah "Sally"

Warneke, Mrs., 162

Washburne, Eli, 75

Welles, Rev. Cornelius, 36, 39, 41, 42, 47
Williams, Sophia W. R., 127
Wilson, Henry, 28, 43, 47, 48–49, 51–52, 76, 94
Wistar, E. M., 125

Women's National Relief Association, 94, 99–100
Women's rights, 4, 11, 60, 79, 103, 111, 135, 161–62

Zimmerman, Hannah, 73

## About the Author

DAVID H. BURTON is Professor of History at St. Joseph's University.